50 SEASONS
A STOKIE
1961 TO 2011

To Sheila and Sarah

Acknowledgements:

Thanks to the Mayor of London, Mr Boris Johnson, for permission to quote him; to Mr Anthony Jones of United Agents for permission to quote from 'Blackadder', to Mr David Croft for permission to quote from 'Dad's Army', and to Stoke City FC for permission to use the photo on the front cover.

My wife Sheila, besides encouraging me throughout, could've given lessons in patience to a room full of saints as she repeatedly showed me how to use Word, save the document and find it again when I kept losing it. Thanks, duck.

And David Lee, author of several fine books on Stoke City, provided some invaluable advice and guidance on getting my script published. So feel free to blame him if you don't like it.

But you can't blame anyone else for any inaccuracies or errors in the text; responsibility for those is mine alone. I've done my best, while relying on my memory stretching back over fifty years (supplemented by Internet research) to be accurate, fair and honest and no negative criticism is intended, explicitly or implicitly, of anyone mentioned, and none should be inferred.

MJ, May 2011

First published in 2011.

Website - www.stokeauthors.co.uk

1961/62 SEASON : Division 2

Rain-macs, toe-caps, collar & tie

M6 under construction

The papers had been full of it all week. There was even a mention on the BBC news. The talk in the potbanks, pits, steelworks, pubs, schools and shops had been of nothing else. It didn't matter that he was older than John Kennedy, the new American president, Stan was coming back home to play for Stoke.

Stoke had been a club on the slide for a while. We'd won only 3 of our first 14 games of this season and the last home gate had barely topped 8,000. But none of this now mattered. It was like a fresh start.

Going to Stan's first game back was a different experience for me and my mate Billy. We'd had to walk to Stoke because the buses had gone past the bus stops full. And when we got near the Victoria Ground the pavements were packed.

Not many people had cars in those days, but we saw our first traffic jam in Stoke.

Then there was the novelty of having to queue at the turnstiles before we were swept by the crowd up the steps at the back of the Stoke End. We pushed and threaded our way down through packed terraces to get to the front. A few Huddersfield fans were mixed in with us, sensing the occasion and looking pleased they'd come.

More people kept pushing their way in and the sounds of optimism and excitement crackled around the stadium. There was no chance of a pie or a cup of tea and the queues for the toilets snaked 50 yards.

Like everybody else, we stood gawping around us. Nearly an hour before kick-off and terraces usually as empty as a drunken promise now heaved with bodies and every seat was taken in the Stands.

A clutch of press photographers and a BBC TV cameraman were already crowded around the players' tunnel.

Nearly 36,000 Stokies eventually filled the ground, more than four times the previous home gate and about 8,000 more than the current capacity of the Britannia Stadium. And nearly everyone had paid at the gate.

Then the press and TV cameraman, who had formed a ring around the tunnel exit, opened up like a guard-of-honour as the players ran onto the pitch. And a roar went into the air that rattled the tea cups in Penkhull.

Defender traumatised by old bloke

Despite the hubbub, Stan loped on to the field looking like the least concerned man on the planet. He only had to touch the ball for the massed Stokies to cheer. And they went mad when he dazzled a Huddersfield defender, then took the ball back and did it again.

And when Stan played a part in setting up a goal he skidded five yards on his knees then pointed to the number 7 on his back... Just kidding.

We won 3-0; our first win in 6 games, but that was only a small part of the story. A balding, middle-aged, slightly built bloke had come back to his ailing home town club and breathed new life into it. This win over Huddersfield in front of a big crowd was no flash in the pan. Things – everything – changed from this day.

We went on to win 12 and draw 4 of our last 25 league games and finish an unexpected 8th in the final table. And Dennis Viollett had joined from Manchester United adding to the feel-good factor that was reflected in average attendances almost doubling to 16,000, even though Stan had missed the first third of the season.

Our Cup exploits had always been the stuff of legend (legendarily awful), but this season we pummelled First Division Leicester 5-2 in front of 38,515 at the Vic in Round 3 of the FA Cup before going out 1-0 at home to a star-studded Blackburn in Round 4 in front of 49,486, a gate we've never bettered for any home game since.

Off the pitch: a big wall, a deep pit and a long road

The M6 motorway from Junction 13 (Stafford & Stone) to Junction 16 (Stoke north) was under construction, as was Europe's deepest pitshaft at Wolstanton. Meanwhile, in Berlin, the East Germans were building a wall which wasn't designed to keep us out of their workers' paradise.

One of our favourite TV shows featured Bootsie and Snudge in *The Army Game.* And a young Clint Eastwood had a starring role as Rowdy Yates in *Rawhide*. Arnold Bennett's birthplace was demolished and Roman pottery artefacts were uncovered in Bucknall.

1962/63 Season: Division 2

Two pits close in the Potteries:

The Place & Victoria Theatre open

It was disappointing. It was even worse than if they'd cancelled 'The Avengers' on Saturday nights and put on more episodes of the Open University starring a seemingly endless procession of blokes with bushy beards. Stoke had been expected to lead the charge for promotion but we'd failed to win any of our first six games. "It is generally known", said Samuel Johnson, "that he who expects much will often be disappointed; yet disappointment seldom cures us of expectation". I reckoned old Sam must've been a Stoke fan.

Worrying times called for drastic measures, so I even started reading stuff other than match reports in my dad's newspaper. It was full of wars, famine, disasters and the 'Cuban Missile Crisis'. It helped to take my mind off things.

But the mood in the Potteries lifted when we won 10 and drew 7 of our next 18 games. Then Tony Waddington pulled off a master stroke. He always seemed to be doing that. He signed the great Jimmy McIlroy to play alongside Stan and Dennis up front. With a front line like that we looked unbeatable.

We lost 6-0 at Norwich in the first game they played together. But *after that* we looked unbeatable, winning six games on the trot. We were now top of the table with only eleven games left to clinch promotion. We drew 0-0 at promotion rivals Sunderland's Roker Park in front of 62,000, won at Cardiff, then beat Sunderland before 42,000 in the return match at the Vic.

My mate Billy said that the next four games were all winnable on paper. But his dad said the games would be played on grass, not paper. Then he gave us a funny look and said "and don't forget, this is Stoke we're on about".

So we lost 3 and drew 1 of the next four games and Chelsea, our biggest promotion rivals, were waiting for us at their place. But Stan and the lads kept cool heads and we won 1-0 in front of 66,199 with a classic goal from Jimmy Mac.

We needed only one win from our last 3 games. We lost the first one at Bury and now had Luton coming to the Vic for our last home game and Southampton away to finish the season off. We could beat Chelsea and Sunderland, no bother, but it was these "easy" games that scared us. This was Stoke we were on about and the shops were running out of toilet rolls.

Where's Pottermouth's dad when you need him?

Jackie Mudie gave us an early lead against Luton, who then dominated the game while we wobbled like jellies on springs. Until Stan settled things down, that is. You can watch it on youtube. He just took control of the situation, waltzed the ball around their 'keeper at the Boothen End goal and made it 2-0. Game over. We were up as Champions. We lost our final game at Southampton and didn't care.

National Footballer of the Year

It's not a case of sentiment; it's a simple fact that nobody else could've had the impact on Stoke's fortunes in the way

Stan did. His presence at the club and performances on the pitch were the catalyst for the resurgence of Stoke City.

And it's not just Stoke fans that held this view; his fellow professionals and national journalists recognised it too as they voted Stan as Footballer of the Year, the first Stoke player ever to win the award.

In just over 12 months since Stan came back Tony Waddington had taken us from a bottom of the Second Division side with a 9,000 average gate to promotion winners with crowds now averaging over 25,000.

Two things then happened in the spring and summer of '63 that seemed to sum up Stoke under Waddo. He arranged for Real Madrid to be the opposition for our Centenary celebration in April. And the players helped to lay extra concreting on the terraces in the close season.

Fab Four in Fab Stoke

The up-and-coming Beatles appeared live at the King's Hall in Stoke.

John Wayne headed a bunch of high profile stars in *The Longest Day*, while Peter O'Toole and David Lean won a sack full of Awards for *Lawrence of Arabia.*

Two of our favourite television shows were *The Saint* and *Z Cars;* the latter reflecting the novelty of our police now being motorised. And *Bonanza* had a catchy theme tune.

Bob Dylan was *Blowin' in the Wind* on our Dansette record player and Nick Hancock was born in Stoke.

1963/64 Season: Division 1

Winkle-pickers & Beatle Cuts;

ABC 'Cine-Bowl' opens in Hanley

Our lads were in new territory and struggling. The odds seemed stacked against them and they must've been desperate at times. But they came through with a combination of courage, discipline and organisation.

So much for the battle of Rourke's Drift that we'd just seen depicted in a film called *Zulu.* We thought that this'd give us an insight into what it'd be like watching Stoke playing against the country's top teams now we're back in the First Division. And, sure enough, in our opening game – to last season's Double winners Spurs – we went a goal down in the first minute. But we came back to win 2-1, with Jimmy Mac scoring both in front of over 40,000 delirious Stokies.

We even featured on the main BBC news that night, a couple of days before Martin Luther King's "I have a dream" speech was broadcast to the world. That's the kind of company we were mixing in now.

Rising star Peter Dobing had joined for a big fee to complement internationals Jimmy O'Niell, Eddie Stuart, Eddie Clamp, Dennis Viollett, Jackie Mudie, Jimmy McIlroy and Stan. And local(ish) lads Ecker Skeels, Calvin Palmer, Bill Asprey and Don Ratcliffe brought the stamina and pace – as did Tony Allen who went on to win England honours. Looking back, this was one of the best footballing teams ever to represent Stoke.

We followed up the win over Spurs with a 3-1 victory at Villa Park. Two games played, maximum points and we were top of the league. Things couldn't be better. It was a steaming-bowl-of-lobby-with-crusty-bread-and-thick-butter moment. Then we came down with a bump as we lost 7 and drew 3 of the next 10 games.

Big John

Waddo recognised that we needed something different and brought in a big youth whose previous experience consisted of playing part-time for non league Kettering Town while (I think) he continued working in a shoe factory.

John Ritchie stormed in and scored 29 league and cup goals (13 in his first 9 games) and finished as top scorer even though he missed the first twelve games of the season.

The Good, the Bad and the Two-Legged Final

From the beginning of December '63 to the end of Feb '64 our league form was grim with only two wins in eleven games.

Yet at the same time we managed to reach the League Cup Final in one of the last years when it was still being played over two legs. It was close, but we lost 4-3 on aggregate to Gordon Banks' Leicester.

But the Cup run seemed to have a positive effect on our league form and we saw out the season in fine style by winning all our games 3-0 against West Ham, Everton, Man United and Liverpool, finishing a comfortable seventeenth in the table.

That's Entertainment

Besides Spurs on the opening day, the stand-out games were when we hammered Ipswich 9-1 (although there were only 16,000 at the Vic to see it as the Grand National was live on TV) and two successive 4-4 home draws with Burnley and Sheffield Wednesday (after we'd been 3-0 and 3-1 up respectively at half-time).

The first season back in the top flight was a see-saw affair, but we played some sublime football and scored a total of 104 goals in all competitions.

The fans clearly saw this both as a season of adventure and one of consolidation and the average league gate of 30,315 (bettered only twice previously, but never bettered since) showed how they appreciated what Waddo and the team had achieved.

A tunnel becomes a chunnel

There was a Great Train Robbery and an Anglo/French agreement to build a channel tunnel. Keele was granted University status.

The Beatles dominated the charts with *'She loves you'* and *'I wanna hold your hand'*. Steve McQueen had star billing in *'The Great Escape'*. Cassius Clay, in his last fight before becoming Muhammad Ali, beat odds-on favourite Sonny Liston to win the World Heavyweight boxing title. And while we were all wide-eyed in disbelief at the news of JFK's assassination in Dallas the first-ever episode of *'Dr Who'* was being aired on the BBC.

And the ABC Cine-Bowl opened in Hanley.

1964/65 Season: Division 1

The Golden Torch opens

Work starts on the A500 'D' road

Dylan was singing *'The times they are a changing'* on the radio and the recent changes for Stoke had been dramatic. Three years earlier we'd lost our opening day home game to Rotherham in front of 11,000 at the Victoria Ground. This year we lost our opening day home game to Everton in front of a massive 43,000.

We followed this up by winning two successive away games before losing at home again. Our form see-sawed much like this for the rest of the season and football again extended our schoolboy vocabulary by teaching us what the word 'inconsistency' meant.

Match of the Day

Like most people, we'd only had a TV in the house for a few years. It was a heavy brown box with a bulbous grey screen and big knobs on the front that made you feel like you were scanning the radar for enemy aircraft when you changed the brightness or volume. And the only football that came on was played between teams wearing various shades of black, white and grey.

The first day we'd had it we marvelled at the grainy picture and even watched ice skating. The FA Cup Final from Wembley was the only game shown live on TV and, other than clips lasting a few seconds on the news, there were no highlights of football matches.

But now we could see "extended highlights" of a top game every week. And the first ever game to be shown was Liverpool v Arsenal in August 1964. Nearly fifty years later, this is still a game that would probably get the first slot on Match of the Day.

On the pitch

After scoring 29 league and cup goals in his first season, John Ritchie showed it wasn't a flash-in-the-pan by doing exactly the same this time round. Four of these were against Sheffield Wednesday at the Vic, following on from his hat trick against them last year.

Dennis Viollett was second top scorer with sixteen league and cup goals. Play-anywhere Calvin Palmer chipped in with eight, and a rare Alan "Bluto" Bloor goal gave us a 1-1 draw at Manchester United.

Home wins over Arsenal and Villa, as well as the away draw at United, had contributed significantly to our consolidation in the top Division.

And the goal-less draw with United in Round 4 of the FA Cup in front of 49,034 at the Vic was another demonstration of the wonder of a game that doesn't need goals to be an epic.

Our final mid-table position of 11th, scoring 67 against 66, with an average home gate of 25,787, represented a good season for us in the top Division.

Stan becomes the first footballer to be knighted

Stan's last ever appearance, and his only one this season, was against Fulham at the Vic five days after his fiftieth birthday.

Not only was he the first footballer to be knighted, he remains (2011) the only player to receive this honour before retiring from playing.

Perhaps it seemed a bit contrived, but Stoke (and football) owed him the honour of this unique farewell. We won 3-1 and he was applauded off the pitch by both sets of players while the crowd roared their appreciation.

Along with Tony Waddington, Sir Stan had orchestrated a transformation of our club in less than four years.

A packed out testimonial game later took place at the Vic in April '65 when Stan's Stoke City All Stars played a World XI which included Yashin, Puskas and Di Stefano. We lost 6-4 and didn't care.

Bottle ovens taken out of use

Winston Churchill died, Nelson Mandela was imprisoned and Gandhi was awarded the Nobel Peace Prize.

Radio Caroline went to sea and *Top of the Pops* was first broadcast by the BBC. The Righteous Brothers *Lost that loving feeling,* the Beatles had *A Hard Day's Night* and the Stones could get no *Satisfaction*. *Dr Zhivago* was on the cinema while *Dr Kildare* was on the telly. And *The Flintstones* was another show with a catchy tune.

Work started on a big dual carriageway running through Stoke on Trent. But there weren't enough fly-overs, roundabouts or tunnels on the A500 'D Road', leaving a problem that had to be dealt with years later. But taking Bottle ovens out of use helped to clean up the air in the Potteries.

1965/66 Season: Division 1

Jack Ashley elected MP

First thing we do every summer when next season's fixture list comes out is to look for whether we've got home games at Christmas and New Year, and at the opposition we'll face at the start of the campaign.

And this time round we were goggle-eyed at the prospect of opening the season with games against Arsenal, Everton, Chelsea (home and away) and Manchester United. But, with the help of new signing Roy Vernon, we did alright - given the calibre of the opposition - in coming out of these first five games with a win, three draws and a defeat.

Although we won 5 of our next 6 games the rest of the season was characterised by steady form as we won nine, drew nine and lost thirteen of our remaining league games.

Highlights of this season (the first in which substitutions were allowed in English football) were our 6-2 hammering of Northampton Town and 4-goal wins over Newcastle and Blackpool.

A couple of seasons of mid-table finishes were just what was needed to stabilise the club at this level. And that's what we got, finishing one place higher this season than last year's eleventh, scoring 65 against 64.

John Ritchie was making a habit of finishing top scorer. He did it again bagging 13 league goals this time round, but these were in only 23 appearances due to niggling injuries.

Peter Dobing added 13 league and cup goals, Harry Burrows and Roy Vernon scored 11 each, and Dennis Viollett added 7 more.

"Wemberley, Wemberley..."

It's difficult for a club the size of Stoke to keep progressing in the top flight. Challenging for the title is usually out of the question, but some fans get bored without the drama of a promotion charge or relegation scrap. So a mid-table finish meant average attendances were again down slightly to 22,503.

We needed a cup run to re-stimulate the interest of these 'occasional' fans, but we didn't get one. Instead, we went out 0-2 at home in the 3rd Round to Third Division Walsall in front of over 32,000.

One of their goals came as a result of us giving away a needless penalty. This is Stoke we're on about.

Future Stokie Geoff Hurst scores

World Cup hat-trick

Sport loves big personalities. Ali could have filled an arena with fans happy just to hear him talk, just like whichever club Jose Mourinho is now managing will accept that the eyes of the media will be on him as much as on the field of play.

England's 1966 World Cup manager Alf Ramsey was, in contrast, a quiet, studious character; more the ship's chaplain than captain. And that's probably why he never really got the full credit his achievement deserved after England won the Jules Rimet Trophy.

Ramsey was a deep thinker about the game, very much like our own Tony Waddington. But the impression I got was that they differed in that Waddo would've had a post-match drink with the players while Alf probably said "well done, chaps" before donning a sensible rain-mac and driving home for a cup of tea.

Ironically it's probably not the winning of the World Cup that is Alf's lasting legacy, as the public is aware that a generous Russian linesman and England having the most talented group of players also played a big part. It's his clever introduction of the 4-4-2 system that has become a standard in world football ever since.

Alf's new formation was brilliantly simple and effective. With two centre-halves (instead of the traditional one) his central defence looked rock solid. And his "wingless wonders" dominated the midfield while leaving opposing full-backs scratching their heads. It was the start of a revolution in football that's seen all sorts of tactical changes since.

Stoke's owrate

Labour Housing Minister Richard Crossman visited the Potteries, tutted a few times and made a statement concluding that "there is nothing in Stoke except the worst of the Industrial Revolution and some of the nicest people in the world".

Clint starred in *'The good, the bad and the ugly'*. And *The Man from UNCLE* and *Star Trek* were among our top TV shows. The Beach Boys felt *Good Vibrations* and The Who sung about *My Generation* at the King's Hall in Stoke.

1966/67 Season: Division 1

Harleys, Lambrettas, Hippies

Arnold Bennett Centenary

Stan's return five years earlier had led to revolutionary change. Now in our fourth season back in the top flight, there were signs of a slower evolution occurring. Local lads Smith, Pejic and Marsh were attracting attention in the reserves but were still some way off being ready for the first team, although young Welshman John Mahoney did make his debut in our 3-0 home win over Sunderland.

Stoke sell leading goal scorer: get used to it

Procol Harum hit the top of the charts with *A Whiter Shade of Pale* and Stoke fans turned a similar hue when John Ritchie, after starting the season with 9 league and cup goals in 15 appearances, was sold to Sheffield Wednesday.

Goal scorers of his calibre are notoriously difficult to replace, but Peter Dobing and Harry Burrows were given extra attacking responsibilities and they rose to the challenge.

Dobing played in more of an out-and-out striker role and ended the season as top scorer with 19 goals; while Burrows, a winger with a hammer of a left foot, came a close second with 17.

Performance of the season was us thrashing the Villa 6-1, with Harry bulging the net with three specials. Low point was us going out to Walsall (again) in the second round of the League Cup. But overall we did okay again this season finishing 12th, scoring 63 against 58 and with average gates up slightly to nearly 26,000.

It's impossible to know, of course, where we would have finished had we hung on to Ritchie and, to his credit, Waddo later acknowledged that he'd wished he hadn't let him go. John went on to score 35 goals in 89 games for Sheffield Wednesday even though he never seemed as home there as he had been in Stoke.

One all-time great leaves, another arrives

Today's footballers (in the new millennium) tend to lead fashion, but not many of our lot took to the pitch on a late 1960s Saturday afternoon looking like they'd arrived on a scooter wearing a parka, or on a Harley and might be covered with tattoos under the red and white stripes.

No sirree: some had let their hair bush out a bit and sported sideboards that came below the ear but that tended to be as far as the boundary was pushed.

England's World Cup winning 'keeper, Gordon Banks, for example, ignoring interest from Liverpool, signed for us in April '67 and with his smart appearance and side-parted hair looked like he could've just come from the courts and left his pin-striped suit and briefcase in the dressing room.

Banksy had arrived just a few weeks before the end of the season and only managed four league appearances. Of these we lost two, drew one and our only victory was against his former club Leicester.

Not an auspicious start, but Waddo had again pulled off a master stroke in bringing the world's best 'keeper to Stoke.

Almost exactly half (36) of Gordon's 73 England caps were awarded while he was a Stoke player.

Big Apple: Light Railway

Morecambe and Wise, The Harry Secombe Show and *Emergency Ward 10* were what we were watching on the TV.

And The Monkees, besides having their own TV series, topped the charts with *'I'm a Believer'*, a popular terraces sing-along for a while.

On the cinema *Bonnie & Clyde* got shot up pretty badly (like they were in real life) and Paul Newman was *Cool Hand Luke.*

Dustin Hoffman and Anne Bancroft starred in The Graduate, for which Simon & Garfunkel provided a fantastic sound track that still passes the test of time.

But *Jungle Book* was the year's top grossing film at the box office.

The television news showed half a million hippies holding a rally in New York's Central Park.

A "rally" seemed to be a word for living in tents, wearing little other than flowers in your hair and sharing "free love" without having to get dressed up and going out on several dates first.

But we didn't care that the Big Apple was reverberating to the excesses of its hippy rally; we had the formation of the Foxfield Light Railway Society.

New York is a long way from Stoke.

18

1967/68 Season: Division 1

'Delilah' tops the charts

Radio Stoke takes to the air waves

The team was still evolving somewhere between the older stars who had taken us up to Division 1 and initially established us there and the next generation of players that were yet to make their mark. But this season still had 'Typical Stoke' written all over it.

We lost exactly half of our 42 league games and, despite having an almost ever-present Gordon Banks between the posts, still managed to concede 73 goals – one of our poorest defensive records for years.

We scored only 50 goals (the lowest for 16 years) as the absence of John Ritchie up front began to tell. Peter Dobing and Harry Burrows again carried the goalscoring burden, finishing the season with 15 each. And Calvin Palmer added 6 from midfield.

One thing that stands out about this season, as is so often the case with Stoke, is the calibre of the opposition for the games we won and lost.

Our fourteen wins included victories over top sides Man City, Spurs, Everton, Leeds and Liverpool as well as pulsating 4-3 wins away to West Ham and Wolves.

Yet we managed to lose to "smaller" clubs (clubs like us) Burnley, Fulham, Sheffield Wednesday, Coventry and really got boing-boinged 3-0 by the Baggies at their place. Our final league position was eighteenth, just avoiding relegation. And we slunk out of the League Cup 2-0 at Leeds and the FA Cup 3-0 at West Ham.

So probably the best that could be said was we had survived another season amongst the elite.

Average attendances had dropped significantly to just under 22,000, a partial reflection of the fact that we lost 16 of our last 25 league games.

Terry Conroy

Clearly what we needed was a skinny, red-headed youth with white legs and a tank full of talent to generate a bit of excitement.

The story goes (I don't know if it's true, but it's a good story I've heard doing the rounds) that Tony Waddington had been tipped off about Terry by a cattle-buyer from Dublin. It's unlikely he sought advice on a young Irish player from a bloke who traded in cows, but that's apparently what he got.

And whatever Tony heard must've been good because he was spurred into action. He watched TC play for Glentoran before sharing a train journey with Terry and persuading him, before they got to wherever they were going, that Stoke was the only club for him. And TC then passed up the chance of signing for Fulham and joined us instead.

Young Terry made only seven appearances in his first season with Stoke, including scoring against Leicester on his debut. But he clearly needed physically building up to cope with top level professional football and was reportedly put on a diet that included big portions of great grub like steak and eggs.

Even so, the brief look we got of him left us in no doubt that Waddo had done it again.

TC had pace, balance, terrific close control, a winner's attitude and nothing fazed him.

If you haven't seen it, have a look on youtube at the goal he scored at Anfield and how he dazzled Chelsea's defenders in the League Cup Final as he developed into his career.

A monument to R J Mitchell

Martin Luther King, named after a man who was instrumental in introducing Protestantism to Europe, was shot dead for trying to introduce more civil rights in America.

Television programmes were broadcast in colour for the first time in Britain. The English smoothie Roger Moore started his final series on TV as *'The Saint',* while the American smoothie Jack Lord started his first in *Hawai 5-0*.

Donovan sang *Mellow Yellow*, The Tremeloes said *Silence is Golden* and Scaffold said *Thank U Very Much*.

On the cinema, Steve McQueen's Frank *Bullitt* gave us the original car-chase and Charlton Heston found himself on *Planet of the Apes*.

Northern Soul music started at the Torch. And over 60,000 people were still employed in the Pottery and allied industries.

And a Spitfire was de-commissioned from service before eventually being put on display at the Museum in Hanley.

1968/69 Season: Division 1

Neil Armstrong on the moon

Ray Reardon over the moon

This season was about patience, endurance, survival and shopping. Some fans weren't patient or prepared to endure Stoke's transitional period. Instead they spent their Saturday afternoons doing things like walking around shops. But they'd have a transistor radio, or would keep asking people for the latest score, or stand staring into a TV shop window.

So the average gate dropped again, this time to below 19,000.

Those that stuck by the team witnessed an incontinence-inducing close encounter with relegation as we finished nineteenth, scoring only 40 goals and conceding 63. But we survived and by the end of the season some significant pieces of the jigsaw were finally dropping in to place.

Experienced centre-forward David Herd had joined from Manchester United giving Waddo some breathing space until he could fill the still-gaping gap left by John Ritchie's departure.

Denis

After a mixed start to the season with 3 wins, 4 defeats and a draw from the first eight games, our next match was at Arsenal's Highbury. We could've been on a hiding to nothing.

So Waddo decided to try something different and played a defence consisting of the world's best 'keeper behind a back four of home grown players. And a young Denis Smith was brought in to partner Alan Bloor, with Jack Marsh and Eric Skeels at full-back.

We went down 1-0, but the manner in which we lost was encouraging. Although he still looked a bit raw it was obvious that Denis was going to be something special. The news people at the time said he looked fearless and was no respecter of reputations. Not like them to understate things. But he wasn't fully ready just yet and, after 3 games, Waddo left him out of the side for a while.

Mickey Pejic made a single appearance late in the season, but then had to bide his time. And Denis made an unhappy return to the side in March '69 for our home game with Leeds who thumped us 5-1.

Our season eventually petered out with Stoke failing to win any of their last six games and taking a 5-0 hammering in the process at Newcastle on the final day. Worse, we had a summer without football to follow.

Marsh, Bloor, Smith, Pejic

But as is so often the case with football, you sometimes have to look beyond a club's results and instead read the trends.

And what we saw this season was the beginning of something that would become special – defenders coming in to the team that would eventually form what was arguably our best ever back four.

Alan Bloor had the solidity of a tank in the middle of our defence. Marsh and Pejic were classic fullbacks who could defend and get forward. And Smithy was in many ways the talisman; the extrovert who led by example and bonded them together.

Ecker Skeels was pushed forward into a defensive midfield role. And all were Stoke through-and-through. While, in front of them, Terry Conroy had by now become a regular and John Mahoney was making his mark.

David Herd finished as top scorer with 9, Peter Dobing bagged 8 and in his first full season TC did well to score 7 from the wing. And there was the relative rarity of an Eric Skeels goal to celebrate on 21st September 1968 when he scored in our 1-1 draw with QPR.

Goaarrn Ray

Robert Kennedy was the latest high profile victim of a political assassination. Neil Armstrong became the first person to step on the moon; or it was, some believe, all a big con trick played on the public by American TV companies – you decide.

Hippies invaded Woodstock and had a great time while Hopper and Fonda starred in the cult movie *Easy Rider*.

The Stones sung about *Honkey Tonk Women* while The Beatles sang *Hey Jude.* Monty Python was first broadcast and Bob Hoskins appeared at our Vic Theatre.

And Stoke's Ray Reardon won the BBC Pot Black trophy, which was the big television tournament at the time.

1969/70 Season: Division 1

Frayed bell-bottoms

Stoke Sixth Form College opens

When average attendances at Stoke suddenly jump by over 5,000 from the previous season then something's happening.

It's not that we were challenging for top of the table; we only came ninth this season. Nor did we ever look like doing anything in the cup competitions.

We'd only scraped past Oxford before going out of the FA Cup to Watford, and went out of the League Cup without scoring a goal.

And they weren't giving away free beer, cheese oatcakes or pies.

But for the first time in three seasons we scored more goals in the league than we conceded (56 against 52). And this was with a team that Waddo had built afresh. A team that was still getting to know each other but supporters could see had potential. A team that defended better with each game, could play football in midfield and trouble any defence.

Signs of a top side emerging

In front of Banks, the home-grown back four of Marsh, Bloor, Smith, and Pejic was now in place. It was a new kind of 'Waddington Wall' consisting of lads that made opposing forwards wish they'd taken up another sport.

And the midfield was rotated around old-timers Skeels, Eastham, Dobing and Burrows who probably tutted and rolled their eyes while young tearaways Mickey Bernard, Josh Mahoney and TC messed about and kept the ball for a laugh.

Then classy forward Jimmy Greenhoff came in from Birmingham. He looked a bargain for £100K, a record for us at the time, as he was the perfect foil for John Ritchie who had come back home from Sheffield Wednesday.

While Big John was an out-and-out striker, Jimmy kept possession under pressure, linked the play between midfield and attack, and scored the type of goals that rarely seemed ordinary.

Mouth-watering. It was like sitting down for cheese oatcakes and brown sauce at breakfast, pie for lunch and lobby for tea every other Saturday.

Perfect. Well, almost.

These things don't happen by accident. To put together a team whose main weakness is simply a lack of games together is either a result of massive spending (you've seen plenty of examples over the years) or a prodigious effort.

But hard work at many levels is only part of it. It takes expertise derived from a certain type of genius, a bit of luck and a willingness to invest and take a risk without putting the club in to serious debt.

No team is ever perfect or can't be improved in some small way, but the one that Waddo had now painstakingly put together was more or less as complete a side that Stoke could assemble.

Highlights and low points

With the players still developing together as a team results were patchy. But we beat Brian Clough's Derby, hammered Sunderland home and away, drew twice against United and Ritchie scored in both games as we did the double over his old club Sheffield Wednesday.

Our worst defeat was a 6-2 mauling at Everton. And for some reason, less than 12,000 turned up to our last home game to see us complete the double over WBA.

Big John resumed his familiar role as top scorer with 16 league and Cup goals, Harry Burrows had a great season and came in second with 14 and Jimmy G got nine.

Eric and Ern

Voting age was lowered from 21 to 18. Simon & Garfunkel built a *Bridge Over Troubled Water* and the great Jimi Hendrix died.

Morecambe & Wise were watched by millions every week on the TV.

Hawkeye and Trapper John were in a *MASH* hospital while *Butch Cassidy and the Sundance Kid* was the first of two big hits for Newman and Redford.

Garth Crooks helped Stoke Schoolboys under-15s to win the Coleman Shield and Pink Floyd appeared at the King's Hall.

1970/71 Season: Division 1

North Staffs Poly opens

The last time we'd reached an FA Cup semi-final (1898/99) Queen Victoria was still on the throne, the manager wore a bowler hat, and the players had handlebar moustaches and lounged around dressed like chain-gang convicts for team photos. But, although we reached the semi-final stage again this season, we didn't go any further than the first time.

The League Cup had been our usual disaster, with us going out in Round Two to Millwall. But we played in *nine* FA Cup games, including replays, in front of crowds totalling over 360,000. That was nearly as many spectators that saw all our 21 home First Division games in the league.

We had our revenge on MIllwall by knocking them out of the FA Cup in the Third Round before playing Huddersfield *three times* in Round Four. Neither penalties nor "golden goals" had yet been introduced so clubs just kept playing replays until there was a winner.

Our first game against them was at the Victoria Ground and finished as a 3-3 draw. They looked a useful outfit led by England forward Frank Worthington. We then drew 0-0 at their place before winning 1-0 with a Jimmy Greenhoff goal in a second replay at Old Trafford, a neutral ground. The three games were watched by 114,000 people.

Ipswich were next up in Round 5; another replay was needed which we won at their place with a Denis Smith goal. We were through to the Quarter Finals and the Potteries was buzzing. A home draw would be great.

To Hull and back

Hull it was, at their place. The tickets went on sale and we dodged off work early only to get to the Vic to find about ten thousand fans queuing up who'd dodged off even earlier. Home and away fans weren't segregated in those days and we could buy tickets for any part of the stadium.

You could say that we hadn't planned things very well because five of us finished up in Billy's dad's Morris 1000 on the road to Hull on match day with tickets for three different parts of the ground. We were part of 15,000 or so Stokies in a huge convoy of buses, Morris 1000s, Ford Anglias, Triumph Heralds and Hillman Minxes that rumbled over the Pennines.

Strangely, none of us felt unusually bothered after we went 2-0 down early in the first half. We just knew it was going to be our day. TC scored just before half-time and the mood changed as even the Hull fans seemed to sense the game shifting away from them. John Ritchie settled the tie by scoring twice in the second half. The pictures are grainy, but you can watch our 3-2 win on youtube. We were in the semis and Cup Fever was spreading.

Oh, crap

You might not know what happened in the semi-final if, say, you're under the age of ten or you've just come out of a very lengthy coma and by some astonishingly long shot this is the first thing you've been given to read. Well, we were 2-0 up against Arsenal at Hillsborough, drew the game in controversial circumstances and lost the replay at Villa Park. Then I failed my driving test the following day. Enough said.

In the league

With the fans' attention and the players' focus being very much on the FA Cup the league was just something to survive this season. We did okay, finishing 13th and scoring 44 against 48. The average crowd was down to just under 20,000 because we were spending our hard-earned on Cup tickets and away travel.

Anyway, undoubted highlight of the season was us beating Arsenal 5-0 at the Vic in front of the MOTD cameras.

New City Library

Decimal Day was 15th February 1971. With 100 pence in the pound instead of 240 pence, all shop prices now finished with 99p instead of 19s 11p.

Ali retained his World Heavyweight title by outscoring Joe Frazier in an epic over 15 rounds at Madison Square Garden.

Clint introduced us to *Dirty Harry,* Gene Hackman was in the first of *The French Connection* epics. And Spielberg made his debut with the brilliantly simple *"Duel".*

Rod's *Maggie May and* John Lennon's *Imagine* became classics, and the Benny Hill show was big on TV.

Freddie Forsyth published *'Day of the Jackal'* (originally rejected by one publisher) and CAMRA was founded.

The City Library was opened in Bethesda Street in Hanley. The average house in the Potteries cost £4,700 and the remains of a Roman fort were excavated in Trent Vale.

1971/72 Season: Division 1

A silver trophy

More fans, the best part of two million, attended Stoke games this season than in any other in our history to date. That's because this was a season like no other in our history. This year was all about the FA and League Cups.

The league

We had an average campaign and, as long as we didn't get relegated, we didn't care. We finished 17th, failed to win any of our last nine games and the few highlights included wins at Arsenal and Manchester City.

The FA Cup

Relatively easy home wins over Chesterfield in R3, Tranmere in R4 and Hull in R5 put us in to the Quarter Finals where we drew 1-1 at Manchester United before beating them 2-1 in a pulsating and dramatic replay at Stoke.

We were in the Semi Finals for the second consecutive season and, like last year, came out of the bag to play Arsenal. We wanted revenge; but what we got was another reminder of how justice can work for the smaller clubs in the bigger games. It doesn't; it just buggers off on holiday.

We got a fortuitous 1-1 draw, courtesy of an Arsenal own goal and, again like last year, faced a replay – this time at Goodison Park.

Jimmy Greenhoff put us 1-0 ahead before Arsenal equalised.

And their winning goal was as bizarre an affair as you're likely to see.

Stoke were playing in an all-white strip. And it was claimed afterwards that some kind of pitch-side salesman wearing a white coat was mistaken for a Stoke player who was playing an Arsenal player on-side. Although well offside he was allowed to score while the game had stopped in disbelief. And that was that; we were out of the cup.

"Things that are hard to bear", according to Seneca, "are sweet to remember". Not in this case.

The League Cup

We played eleven games just to get to the Final. These included a replay in Round 3 to get past Oxford and two replays in Round 4 to overcome Manchester United (again).

We were involved in another four games to get past West Ham in the Semis – although, as the Duke of Wellington said at Waterloo, it was "the nearest run thing you ever saw in your life".

At one point it looked like we were going out to the Hammers in the second leg at their place. Winger Harry Redknapp lost Mickey Pejic and ghosted in to the right side of our box. Gordon brought him down and gave away a penalty. But Banksy redeemed himself by making his best save ever (even better than the one from Pelé) and palmed the Geoff Hurst spot kick over the bar.

West Ham put up a great fight but we eventually got through to meet Chelsea in the Final before 97,852, the biggest crowd ever for a Stoke game.

TC gave us an early lead at Wembley; Peter Osgood equalised, but mighty George Eastham scored the winner. The ball was loose and George jabbed it... with his toe...from two yards.... over the line ... into the net! The final score was 2-1 and...

We'd won our first ever major trophy!

We shouted ourselves hoarse, cheered, sang and laughed. Some cried; others just stood still and tried to take it in.

It was the Fourth of March, Nineteen Seventy-Two.

An estimated half a million people, virtually the whole population of North Staffordshire, lined the streets the following day to welcome the team home with the trophy. Everyone who was there would like it to happen again so that a new generation of Stokies could have the same experience.

And Gordon Banks became the second Stoke player to win the national Footballer of the Year Award.

Duelling banjos, a horse's head and UFOs

The first of *The Godfather* epics hit the cinemas. And Burt Reynolds and Jon Voight starred in *Deliverence*.

Elton John sang *Rocket Man* and the nation's favourite TV show was the Eurovision Song Contest.

The M6 and M1 motorways were connected, providing a direct route to London for the first time. Maxims nightclub in Newcastle was listed as a Grade II building and two Police constables reported seeing UFOs over Stoke on Trent.

1972/73 Season: Division 1

Heavy Metal & Glam Rock

Unity House built in Hanley

"Man's greatest joy", according to Genghis Khan, was to "slay his enemy, plunder his riches, ride his steeds and embrace his women".

If he'd been born in Stoke around the same time as me I'd be willing to bet that although he might not have got a job with Social Services, he'd have been happy enough with us winning the League Cup last season.

We were happy; some success at last had brought happiness. But success re-defines everything; the bar has now been set higher for this season.

And given that it took 108 years to win our first major trophy it would be unlikely that we could repeat the feat in successive seasons, so a period of stability was needed while Waddo and the club took stock of their options.

Two good signings

West Ham and England World Cup hero Geoff Hurst, who could probably have had his pick of the top teams, joined us along with speedy Scottish international winger Jimmy Robertson.

They boosted our attacking options alongside Ritchie, Greenhoff and Conroy.

Two great losses

Only seven months after they had played their part in our League Cup win at Wembley both Gordon Banks and Peter Dobing, who had each made only eight appearances this season had to retire from the game. Gordon tragically lost an eye in a road accident after a heroic display at Anfield.

And Peter never fully recovered from a broken leg.

The league campaign

John Farmer became Stoke's regular 'keeper and we had a solid rather than spectacular season, finishing 15th and scoring 61 against 56.

We'd got off to a slow start winning only one of our first nine games before we thumped Man City 5-1 at the Vic, one of the highlights of our season.

Our next two games were away from home and were remarkable for the fact that we scored 3 in each and yet still lost both. The scores were 5-3 at Wolves and 4-3 at Spurs.

Results then see-sawed through the middle of the season but we finished strongly with 6 wins in the last 8 games. And the bonus was local lad Alan Dodd making three appearances in defence, but wasn't yet ready for a regular spot.

Just for once Big John didn't finish as top scorer. He came in second with 16 league and cup goals, Geoff Hurst scored 13, but Jimmy Greenhoff topped the list with 20.

Meanwhile, we were back to normal in the Cup competitions, going out early to Man City and Notts County.

The cream of Europe

We had qualified for the EUFA Cup and could look forward to playing one of Europe's elite. Then we drew Kaiserslautern out of the hat. I'd never heard of them before and I guess that they might never have heard of Stoke either. We were at home for the first leg; Kaiserslautern didn't look up to much and we ran out comfortable winners at 3-1.

Me and Billy were out on the night of the second leg. We went back to his house and asked his dad how Stoke were doing. "Losing 4-0, last I heard". And he reckoned Big John had been sent off less than a minute after coming on as a substitute.

Great. Our European campaign had met with the same success as those of Napoleon and Hitler; we just hadn't hung around as long as they had.

No flights from Meir

Britain joined the EEC; a move that still has major implications for all of us today (2011).

Redford and Newman had their second big hit with *The Sting* while Jack Nicholson played a bad ass sailor in *The Last Detail*. And the chaps with wizard prang moustaches became TV stars as they planned their escape from *Colditz.*

Slade hit number 1 with *Cum on feel the Noize* and glam rockers Led Zeppelin and Ziggy Stardust appeared live at Trentham Gardens and the Victoria Hall respectively. And Rod sang *You Wear it Well.*

And the aerodrome at Meir was closed.

1973/74 Season: Division 1

Glitter boots & Flares: Stoke Film Theatre opens

Ten years of consolidation in the top flight, our first major trophy and a reputation for playing entertaining football. Our highest league placing since we were promoted was ninth and the safe money was on another mid-table finish.

Yep; this is where we should yawn and stretch at the prospect of another run of the mill season. But one of the things that make the game interesting is its unpredictability.

And that's especially the case with Stoke. We're the white-water rafters of football with a punctured dinghy and a sticking plaster.

Relegation or Europe?

One win in the first 12 games and things don't look good. After 24 games it's six wins and nine draws: a bit better, but we were still hovering just above the relegation zone.

George Eastham retired after making only two appearances, and with Peter Dobing retiring the previous season we were lacking some vision and craft in the centre of the park.

Huddy: Kings Road to Campbell Road

Some things, although true, still seem barely believable. Like the fact that all our domestic dogs have evolved from wolves. Or that a high-profile London-born playboy would leave Chelsea's fashionable Kings Road, and the Smoke to fill the void in Stoke's midfield. But both these things happened.

Waddo was good at making the unlikely happen at Stoke; and he did it again when he shelled out a record £240K to install the peerless Alan Hudson as our playmaker.

And it's not over-stating the case to say that Huddy's impact on our results was not far from that of Stan's a decade earlier. In fact, Huddy comes second only to Stan on my list of Stoke Greats that I've seen over the years.

The Stoke team that struggled to win was transformed in to one that won 9, drew 7 and lost only 2 of its last 18 matches as Huddy dominated games while oozing that seemingly effortless class.

His debut in our 0-0 home draw against Liverpool had Shanks drooling. His goal in our comeback from 2-0 down to beat Don Revie's Leeds 3-2 helped to end their record-equalling unbeaten run.

And his winner against former club Chelsea at Stamford Bridge was preceded by our win over Spurs and followed by our defeat of Manchester United on the last day of the season.

"A season of two halves"

Pundits like to use this kind of cliché, but the pedant in me would more accurately say that it was "a season of four-sevenths and three-sevenths".

Had our form continued as it was during the first four-sevenths the likelihood is we would've been relegated. Or had it been all the way through as it was for the final three-sevenths we would've won the title. That's a measure of the impact Huddy had.

As it happened, we ended the season in 5th place, our highest league placing since finishing 4th in 1946/47. And we had qualified for European football next season.

John Ritchie resumed his usual position as top scorer with 14 league and cup goals (including a hat-trick against Southampton) with Geoff Hurst scoring 12.

And although Jimmy Greenhoff scored what was for him a modest nine goals, it was his link play with Huddy, based on a seemingly uncanny understanding between them, which sparked and fuelled the team's transformation.

The Cups

We went out of the League Cup to Coventry and the FA Cup to Bolton, both early doors. Enough said.

"Don't tell him, Pike"

New Year's Day became a public holiday for the first time. Des O'Connor and Tommy Cooper hosted the top TV shows.

An Italian defender was baffled by a "Cruyff turn" in the World Cup. Abba won Eurovision with *Waterloo*.

And *Godfather II* and *Blazing Saddles* are about as different as you could get.

Dad's Army was the top TV show. And Bachman-Turner Overdrive sang *You Ain't Seen Nothing Yet* as streakers skipped over the net at Wimbledon's centre court and leaped over the wicket at Lords.

And Robbie Williams was born in Tunstall.

1974/75 Season: Division 1

Kevin Keegan perms

Gladstone Pottery Museum opens

It's as likely in the new millennium that a club outside the select few will win the league title as it is President Obama getting a Christmas card off the Taliban.

But the mid '70s was still a time before a handful of the big city clubs unashamedly bought the trophies. Smaller clubs like Stoke, Derby and Ipswich could still attract enough top players to challenge for silverware.

And in 74/75 that's exactly what happened. Clough and Taylor's Derby won the title, Ipswich came third and we were fifth, only four points off the top.

Chelsea were relegated and would be replaced by 2nd Division champions Manchester United the following season.

It's only human nature to consider the "if only" we'd managed another win and two more draws and won our first title, but pointless to dwell on it. The fact is we'd played some great football, scoring 64 against 48, and average attendances were up to a healthy 27,000.

It was a terrific season, other than for one horrible injury.

End of Big John's career

Quality left winger Geoff Salmons had joined pre-season, Alan Dodd came in for the injured Alan Bloor and the team had a very solid look about it as we trounced Leeds 3-0 on the opening day. Early season results had been a bit mixed by the time we went to Ipswich for our ninth game.

Then disaster struck as John Ritchie had his leg broken and, although we didn't know it at the time, his career ended.

John had scored 4 goals in his 7 appearances to date, this being par for the course as he averaged a goal every other game. Since joining us a decade earlier he had scored 171 goals in 343 appearances and remains to this day (2011) Stoke's all-time record scorer.

And with the 35 goals John scored in his spell with Sheffield Wednesday he joined the elite group of players to have scored over 200 goals, and nearly all in the top flight.

Peter Shilton

Tony Waddington now had a relatively inexperienced 'keeper at the back and had lost his top scorer up front. So he gambled and paid a world record fee for a goalkeeper in November '74 when he signed Leicester and England international Peter Shilton for £350K.

It's worth saying again: *Stoke paid a world record fee for a goalkeeper.* Peter's signing dominated the headlines for a while and picked everybody up after the loss of JR.

Goals

There were some terrific performances this season. The TV cameras were at Birmingham to record our comprehensive 3-0 win, as they were at the Vic for our 4-0, Huddy-inspired, trouncing of Man City. We won 2-0 at Spurs before beating

Liverpool 2-0 and Chelsea 3-0 at the Vic. We also beat Chelsea 6-2 in an FA Cup replay which (I think) was our first Sunday match at the Victoria ground.

Although we might have expected another 15 goals from John Ritchie if he'd stayed fit we didn't do too bad with Greenhoff finishing top scorer with 14, Huddy got 10, Salmons & Robertson bagged 8 each and, amazingly, TC scored 10 in only 11 games (as well as a hat-trick in the FA Cup) in an injury-plagued season.

Finishing 5th in '73/74 meant that we'd qualified for this season's EUFA Cup and we were drawn against the mighty Ajax; Cruyff, Neeskins, Repp, the lot. We matched them comfortably over two legs with Huddy at his imperious best; a measure of our quality at the time.

It was a two-leg tie and a 1-1 draw in the first leg at Stoke was followed by a goal-less draw in Amsterdam. So they went through on the Away Goals Rule.

Tricky Dickie & Ronald McDonald

Nixon resigned over Watergate. Ali beat Grill salesman George Foreman in the "Rumble in the Jungle".

Jaws was another brilliantly simple and effective plot by Steven Spielberg. And Jack Nicholson won an Oscar for *One Flew Over the Cuckoo's Nest.*

The Bay City Rollers had teeny-boppers wearing plaid. *Fawlty Towers* and *The Sweeney* topped the TV charts.

Gerald Seymour's *Harry's Game* was a best-seller and Britain's first McDonalds opened in Woolwich, East London.

1975/76 Season: Division 1

Bradeley-born cricketer David Steele

made his England debut

We all make plans, whether it's for today, this week, this year or for the longer term future. Yet it's often the case that the biggest changes in our lives result from major and unexpected events that occur out of the blue on an ordinary weekday when nothing much in particular is happening.

This season was characterised by one such event.

Although it wasn't immediately evident to us fans at the time, the most significant thing that happened this season was when the Butler Street Stand roof collapsed in a gale on 2nd January 1976; thankfully when nobody was in it

Middling sort of season: Double over Arsenal

Ian Moores was a big local lad who looked promising up front, scoring 11 goals in 29 appearances. But he had the hard task of playing the target-man role previously performed by former favourites John Ritchie and Geoff Hurst.

And the team was badly affected by injuries this season with Smithy, Jimmy Robertson, TC and Huddy missing a lot of games between them. In fact, Peter Shilton was our only ever-present.

We finished 12th, scoring 48 against 50, and our average gate was down by nearly 5000.

It's an insight into where Stoke was at the time when a 12th place finish could be described as an anti-climax yet results included a double over the Gunners, 3-2 wins against Leeds and Everton, and a 1-0 victory over United at Old Trafford, courtesy of a rare Alan Bloor goal.

And although the records show a 1-0 home win over a Middlesbrough side that included Graeme Souness on 17th January '76, the game was actually staged at Vale Park as workmen were still pulling what was left of the roof off the Butler Stand seats.

The FA Cup run was decent. We beat Spurs and Man City before going out to Sunderland by a lucky (for them) deflection at their place.

The League Cup was a different story. We were drawn at Lincoln and you can guess the rest.

Eric "Ecker" Skeels and Garth Crooks

A great club servant and a fan favourite, Ecker made his final appearance for Stoke on 21st February '76 in our 2-1 home defeat to Spurs.

This quiet, solid, reliable, talented and versatile player made a total of 592 appearances in his long career with Stoke – more than any other player.

One of a rare breed was Ecker.

A few weeks after Ecker took his final bow, young local lad Garth Crooks made his debut in our 1-0 home defeat by Coventry.

The story goes that Crooksy had been annoying Stoke manager Tony Waddington by continually kicking a ball against the outside of his office wall. Kids, eh?

So Waddo solved the problem by bringing him into the club as an apprentice. Did Waddo then get his own back on Garth by making him write "cost kick a bow ginst a wow yed eet back and bost eet?" a hundred times? Nah; don't suppose so.

Stand roof not insured

I'm not going to be wise after the event and claim that I could see the implications for Stoke when the news came out that the Butler Street Stand roof was uninsured. I didn't, and I don't think many of us did.

But the eventual consequences were dire for next season and beyond.

Another epic fight

Ali beat Frazier in what was billed the "Thrilla in Manila".

Hoffman and Redford investigated *All the President's Men,* Robert Di Nero was a New York *Taxi Driver* and Stallone began the *Rocky* legend that's still going over thirty years later.

W*hen the Boat Comes In,* starring the brilliant James Bolam, topped the TV charts and *The Two Ronnies* was a Saturday night favourite.

And the open air swimming pool at Trentham Gardens closed before the hottest summer for decades.

1976/77 Season: Division 1

Two more Pits close in the Potteries

Picture this: you're a recently retired player, forced out of the game early through injury after barely making a ripple on the surface of your profession. You're on the coaching staff of a Second Division club with a once-proud history, but it's now on the slide. The manager's post has become available and you want it, but there's no money to spend and the group of players you've inherited are struggling around the relegation zone.

And if you take them down you'll be the person for ever associated with Stoke's demise.

So, do you take on the job? Run a mile? Or run several miles?

That's the position Tony Waddington found himself in 15 years earlier. Unfortunately in those days there were no Internet football message boards from which he could access expert advice. He had to learn the job the hard way, as he was going along.

His first task was to save Stoke from relegation. His next was to save us from relegation again. He did.

Then he got us promoted, fielded a group of fabulous players, established us as a First Division club with a reputation for entertaining football, took us (twice) on an FA Cup odyssey, took us into Europe, and won the League Cup.

Then he had to sell some of his best players, had a bad season and was pressured in to resigning.

The real cost of the Stand roof

No doubt Waddo, like the fans, didn't want to sell his best players to cover the cost of re-building the Butler Street Stand roof. But it seems like that's what happened. Sean Hazelgrave and Ian Moores were sold pre-season, but the £110K they raised wasn't enough.

So 14 games into the season Jimmy Greenhoff was sold to Manchester United. Alan Hudson went to Arsenal a couple of weeks later and was soon followed out of the club by Mickey Pejic going to Everton. And it felt to us fans as though the heart had been ripped out of the team.

Some fans thought it was a case, to paraphrase Oscar Wilde, of the Board knowing the price of players but not their value to the club. Others thought – and my guess is this was probably more likely - that they had no option but to sell. Only the people in charge at the time would know for sure.

But what I do know is that it was Waddo who was the target of the fans' frustration while chants of "Waddington out" rang round an increasingly angry and agitated Victoria Ground as team morale and performances collapsed under the pressure.

Relegation

We finished the season second bottom with 34 points, scoring 28 against 51 and average crowds had dropped to 19,000. Garth Crooks finished as our leading scorer with six goals, while TC came in second with five.

We weren't relegated with games still to play, so there was a glimmer of hope for us on the last day in our away game to

Villa. We needed to win and for other results to go our way. But former Sky Sports presenter Andy Gray, partnered by future Stoke manager Brian Little, scored their winner and sent us down.

At the moment we went down George Eastham was actually in charge as team manager. Tony Waddington had resigned some weeks earlier following our home defeat to Leicester as the pressure on him had become intolerable.

It was a sad way for him to go and the club later took steps to redeem his memory by commemorating Tony's name in and around the Britannia Stadium.

Personal Computers for all

and a Personal toilet for one

Peanut farmer Jimmy Carter became president of the United States. And how many of us took much notice when the world's first ever desktop PC was demonstrated in Chicago?

Richard Dreyfus had a *Close Encounter of the Third Kind* and *Star Wars* continued our collective obsession with life elsewhere. Red Rum won the Grand National for the third time.

Impressionist Mike Yarwood and *Sale of the Century* smoothie Nicholas Parsons hosted our favourite TV shows. Fleetwood Mac released *Rumours* while the Bee Gees were all bushy hair and beards with *Saturday Night Fever*.

And the Duke of Edinburgh was allocated his own personal toilet on his night out at Jollees.

1977/78 Season: Division 2

Steel production ends at Shelton Bar

Football is the same game no matter where or when it's played. But the differences in *how* it's played were suddenly more noticeable to us Stoke fans when, after more than a decade in the top flight, our club had been relegated to the Second Division.

The same game was played by a different kind of player, at a different pace and in a different way. And nobody was going to help the new boys who thought that they were temporarily down on their luck and didn't really belong here.

There's no easy way back to the top Division, so a club has to learn how to survive in its new surroundings. That can take a while and after donkey's years of stability under Waddo we were in new territory in more ways than one.

George Eastham enjoyed legendary status for being the scorer of our cup-winning goal at Wembley. But George didn't enjoy the same level of success as our manager. He'd won only one of his 13 games in charge last season and despite bringing in Howard Kendall, a classy, industrious midfielder, he struggled to do much better this time round.

The league campaign

After an opening day defeat at Mansfield our form picked up and we won our next two games. Then Peter Shilton, who, to his credit, had stuck with us throughout our relegation season, left us (after 120 appearances) to return to the top flight with Derby.

Roger Jones came in to replace him and featured in 5 draws and a 4-0 win for us against Sheffield United before he experienced being on the losing side.

But our form then dipped with 9 defeats in our next 15 games and George was sacked. He was replaced by Alan A'Court, who was in charge for one league game and one FA Cup game, and we lost both.

So then, with three months of the season remaining and promotion looking unlikely, the Board brought in another Alan as manager – former Derby and Wales midfielder Alan Durban, who was still cutting his teeth in management.

Alan came across as being a no-nonsense character, although this was probably just what the club needed at the time. And his methodical and pragmatic approach settled things down.

Crucially he did something about our lack of a target man up front by bringing in Brendan O'Callaghan, who scored with his first touch of the ball after coming on as a substitute on his debut. After that, we called our goldfish "Big Bren".

We eventually finished the season in 7th position, scoring 51 goals against 49. But the average gate had dropped to 15,000, just over half what it had been three years earlier.

Garth Crooks was now an established regular and finished as top scorer with 19 league and Cup goals, including a hat-trick against Blackburn.

And Howard Kendall got 7 goals while Brendan O'Callaghan made an encouraging start with 6 in 13 appearances.

The Cup campaigns

Bristol City had knocked us out of the League Cup in the Second Round, but we'd breezed past non-league Tilbury by 4-0 in R3 of the FA Cup.

We then had the good fortune to get another home draw against non-league opposition at the Vic in the Fourth Round.

But this is Stoke we're on about and the game finished with a 3-2 victory to Blyth Spartans, who were cheered off the Victoria Ground pitch by a sporting Stoke crowd after their historic victory.

Alan Bloor

This quiet, but hugely talented defender made the last of his 470 appearances in a Stoke shirt in our 1-0 defeat to Burnley.

Alan's centre-back partnership with Denis had been the stuff of a Stoke legend.

Elvis

Elvis died and Bjorn Borg won Wimbledon for the third year in a row.

Superman made sure we've got a film to watch on TV at Christmas.

Travolta and Newton-John posed and pouted in *Grease*.

Di Nero starred in *The Deer Hunter*. And *The Muppet Show* was big with the kids on TV.

And Jonathan Wilkes was born in Baddeley Green.

1978/79 Season Division 2

Kaftans & Leg warmers

Stoke's Arthur Berry wins Radio Award

There always has been, still is, a tension between entertaining football and "functional" football. The first can be great to watch, but might not get the results supporters want. The second is about getting results, but sometimes you might as well watch them coming in on ceefax.

Go home happy after watching your team lose a thriller 4-3? Or win 1-0 after they've re-defined the concept of tedium? The ideal, of course, is to play entertaining football that gets results.

What's so difficult about that? This: you need a top manager who is backed by the Board and a great set of players, with strength in depth for every position. And luck; because professional football exists in a highly competitive atmosphere and what Stoke wants is no different to what every other club wants.

Alan Durban had taken Stoke on when we were at a low ebb and still sinking. He'd stabilised the club last season then put together a solid side for this year's campaign. He brought in the classy and assured Mike Doyle to play alongside Smithy, and they patrolled our defence like a couple of Mob enforcers. He ignored the grumbling of some Stoke fans about midfielder Sammy Irvine, even threatening to make him captain if it carried on. And after bringing in striker Paul Randle ordered Garth Crooks to play out of his normal position on the left wing.

Then this disciplinarian, who did things his way and didn't court popularity, got us promoted back to the top flight.

Start with a 1-0: finish with a 1-0

The early signs were good as we won 5 and drew 3 of our first eight games. We were the Division's "steady Eddies" for most of the season, losing only 6 games.

Brendan had finished as our top scorer with 15 and Garth came in second with 12. But although we weren't as free-scoring as some sides, we didn't need to be as our defence was tighter than a duck's sphincter and we kept clean sheets in exactly half our games. And our goal difference of plus 27 was better than any other Stoke team had managed in well over thirty years.

But we still went into the last game of the season, away to Notts County, unsure of promotion. There were no play-offs yet and the top three clubs went up automatically.

Depending on results elsewhere, a draw might've been enough for us. But news came through late in the game that we needed to win. And Paul Richardson, who had scored our winner in the 1-0 away to Cambridge on the opening day, rounded off both the game and the season nicely by scoring our late winner on the final day.

A passer-by outside the ground would've thought it was Notts County who had scored as around three-quarters of the 21,579 in the stadium erupted. But it was the Stoke fans who had taken over for the day.

When we'd got promoted under Waddo in the '60s we'd almost expected it. But not this time: after the way we'd started in the Second Division the previous season we'd looked more likely to get relegated than promoted. Celebrations last time had been wholly euphoric. This time it was raw happiness based on a feeling of disbelief, like you'd had a phone call saying you'd won the pools after a bad day at work.

Alan Durban had come up with a pretty good compromise where the football had been decent *and* had got results. But I'm not sure whether some of us at the time really gave Durban the credit he deserved – a situation that would be echoed years later under Tony Pulis.

But, like the style or not, we were up! And we had signed a young goalkeeper named Peter Fox who looked promising.

TC

Terry Conroy had made only 3 starts and 4 appearances as substitute all season. He'd given his all for Stoke over the years and packed it in in April '79 after injuries had taken their toll. Another good un gone.

Super Seb

Maggie became our first female PM. Seb Coe set new World Records over three distances, and all within 41 days.

Hollywood, as ever, reflected, or roused, depending on your view, our collective fears with *The China Syndrome, Apocalypse Now* and *Alien*. As an antidote, Larry Grayson's *Generation Game* was the nation's favourite TV show.

And The Doulton Story featured at the V&A museum.

1979/80 Season: Division 1

Big shoulder pads

St Joseph's School re-opens in Trent Vale

A Spartan leader once listened to the threat made by his enemy. "If we take the city by force", said the invaders' messenger, "all your women and children will be killed and the men used as slaves for the rest of their lives".

The Spartan's laconic reply was "*If*".

It's a small word with, as Kipling's poem demonstrated, huge implications. And it's a word that was often used by Stoke fans around this time when we talked about what the club could achieve *if* we hung on long term to our developing players.

By the end of this season Alan Durban had drafted in half a team of relatively untried youngsters to play alongside old warhorses like Smith, Doyle, Richardson and O'Callaghan. But there was no need for concern about bringing in so many young lads together; these were a talented bunch.

The four outfield players all went on to win international honours, while the goalkeeper eventually put himself in the Stoke City record books.

Crooks, Heath, Chapman, Bracewell and Fox

England U21 international Garth Crooks was now an established regular up front and was joined from the outset by fellow Stokie Adrian (Inchy) Heath (soon to be another

U21 England player) who went on to make 32 appearances and score 5 goals in his first season.

Lee Chapman, who also won U21 caps, was the next of our young local lads to make the line-up, coming into the side in December '79 before going on to score 3 goals in 14 appearances.

Then Paul Bracewell became the last of this crop of youngsters to emerge from the youth ranks and break into the first team when he made his debut at Wolves a couple of months before the end of the season. Paul eventually won three full England caps to complement his U21 collection.

And, although we couldn't have known it at the time, Peter Fox took over in goal from Roger Jones halfway through the season and would go on to make a total of 477 appearances for Stoke – more than any other goalkeeper in our history.

The league campaign

Not only was the team obviously going through a major re-structuring, it also had to face better quality opposition every week since being promoted.

So performances were mixed with inevitable periods where we struggled. But we did okay and finished 18th in the table, scoring 44 goals against 58. And average crowds just topped 20,000.

For a side in transition, trying to embed several youngsters, there were some inevitable maulings. We lost easily at Leeds, Wolves, and Man United. But we had good wins over Spurs, Villa, Middlesbrough and did the double over West Brom.

The Cups

We went straight out of the FA Cup with a 1-0 defeat at Burnley. But we did play four games in the League Cup, albeit two of these were replays. After drawing with Swansea at the Vic we won the replay at their place.

But lightening doesn't strike twice: in the next Round we drew with Swindon at the Vic and lost the replay at their place. This is Stoke we're on about.

Borg

The American presidential election campaign was underway and it was reported that the ABC (Anybody But Carter) movement was gaining ground.

Borg won Wimbledon for the fifth successive year.

Bands with the definite article in their name, The Clash / The Jam / The Damned, played at the Victoria Hall. Queen topped the charts with *Another One Bites the Dust.*

And Jim Hacker hadn't yet reached the top of the greasy political pole when *Yes Minister* appeared on TV.

Life began to imitate art again when the Ewing women in the American super-soap *Dallas* set new trends in fashion and the shoulder pad industry revitalised the economy.

The *Antiques Roadshow* visited Stoke on Trent, the World Darts Championship was held at Jollees in Longton and what was to become one of our best performing schools re-opened in Trent Vale.

1980/81 Season: Division 1

Lycra & aerobics: City Museum opens in Hanley

Billy said some people in London thought it was "cool" to eat sushi which, he'd been told, is raw fish. He wondered why they didn't take it home and cook it properly first, like we do in Stoke. And it was for reasons like this we felt sorry for any player leaving Stoke for the capital.

Garth Crooks was the latest, moving to Spurs pre-season for a big fee. Billy said that Crooksy would have to make do without cheese oatcakes and lobby. And we all sensed Billy's pain.

Denis missed the entire season with his latest spate of injuries. So Brendan moved to centre-back while Lee Chapman and Inchy Heath formed the front pair. Peter Fox became our ever-present 'keeper throughout the season.

And young winger Loek Ursem worked hard to establish himself, making 24 appearances, plus four as a substitute and finished with 7 goals, making him joint second-top scorer with Brendan.

Send in the Clowns

Results in the opening weeks of a season are often all over the place until form settles down and clubs get into the groove. Newly promoted sides are usually buzzing, far more than their opponents who've seen it all before. So we get anomalies like a relatively small club leading the table after a couple of games.

Even so, we weren't expecting an opening-day 5-1 tonking by Norwich at their place, or to draw our first two home games then follow this up with another 5-0 thrashing at Nottingham Forrest. Twelve goals conceded and we only had two points on the board after four games.

And after an ultra-defensive performance against Arsenal, some brave, or misguided, journalist questioned our style of play.

We've all been there; things aren't going great and you feel like you would if the dog had puked on the expensive new carpet after stealing your sausage roll and the telly wasn't working. Then, just to make your day, somebody can't resist giving you a poke with the verbal equivalent of a cattle prod.

Alan Durban's well-reported reaction to this impertinence was along the lines of inviting the reporter to go and watch a bunch of clowns if he wanted entertaining.

But things did pick up after this poor start.

Our form improved and we finished 11th in the table - seven places higher than last season. But we'd sold a top young striker and drawn 18 of our 42 league games, so our average gate dropped by nearly a quarter to 15,580

But Lee Chapman was beginning to look the business up front. He made 41 appearances in the number 9 shirt. And his 17 league and Cup goals included two hat-tricks.

Trouble is, this is Stoke we're on about and goalscoring strikers don't tend to hang around for long nowadays.

Off to the Black Cats

Alan Durban left Stoke at the end of the season to manage Sunderland. He'd introduced greater organisation to our play, had won promotion and stabilised Stoke in a higher Division. But fans want to see a winning side and there'd been too many draws so crowds were down.

Not for the first time (and certainly not for the last) Stoke fans were left arguing about where the balance between getting results and providing entertainment should lie.

Ian Botham: a cricketing giant

Charles and Di got married, Ronald Reagan became the US president and John Lennon was shot dead in New York.

The wreck of the Titanic was discovered in very deep water.

Borg finally lost to somebody (McEnroe) at Wimbledon. Steve Davis won the World Snooker title.

And Ian Botham inspired one of the most dramatic sporting performances in history when the England cricket team turned the tables on the Aussies to win the Ashes. At one point the odds on England winning were around 500-1.

Raiders of the Lost Ark and *Chariots of Fire* (which won an Oscar for its British writer) were the top films. And *The Hitch-Hiker's Guide to the Galaxy* was a television hit.

Meanwhile, Del, Rodders and granddad were convinced that *Only Fools and Horses* (work) in their first ever series on TV.

1981/82 Season: Division 1

First Potteries Marathon

The mandarins at the Football Association decided to spice things up a bit and introduced a new rule to promote attacking football; 3 points instead of 2 for a win. They thought the game had become too defensive and negative.

It's easier to defend than attack and defenders tend to be a lot cheaper to buy in the transfer market. An average of a point per game usually guaranteed a safe mid-table finish so there was insufficient incentive to play attacking football and win matches.

And if they were looking for a positive reaction from clubs like Stoke, it looked like they got it when we kicked off the season with a surprise 1-0 win at Arsenal and followed up by thumping Coventry 4-0 at the Vic. Two games played and we were top of the league with 6 points.

Alan Durban's former assistant Richie Barker had been promoted to the managerial role. And we all hoped that Richie was the man to consolidate our place in this Division. But Stoke were now playing top-flight football and survival was about as much as we could've expected at this time. And after a slow start, Richie led us to survival – just.

We scraped a single point from the next five games before a terrific performance and a 3-1 home win over Everton. But we then lost 6 of the next 10 games we played to the end of December. We were now almost halfway through the season and struggling with only 17 points on the board.

And then one of our brightest young prospects, Adrian Heath, was sold to Everton for £700K.

Sammy McIlroy & Steve Bould

Although Dave Watson, former England centre-back, was near to the end of his career, he was brought in to add experience and composure to the defence. And Sammy Mac, a Northern Ireland international, was a real coup; he still had plenty in the tank and brought class, experience and energy to our central midfield.

Lanky, Blurton-born lad Steve Bould had made a couple of brief appearances at right-back and then disappeared back into the Reserves without giving much indication of the top class centre-half he'd eventually become. And Rod Stewart look-alike Alan Biley, a busy and industrious sort of player with some flair, also came in and kept the crowd entertained with his hair styles.

But despite these new players we were clearly in trouble. At one point we lost 8 and drew 1 of nine consecutive games and only avoided relegation by winning the last game of the season, finishing 18th, and scoring 44 against 63. We ended up with the same number of wins (12) as last season, but suffered 10 more defeats than last time. It was clear that a number of other clubs had adapted better than us to the three points for a win Rule.

Not only that, we had already allowed two of our England U21 forwards, Crooks and Heath, to leave and then another, Lee Chapman, top scorer again with 17, moved to Arsenal as soon as the season ended. Great.

Denis the Legend

On 20th May 1982 Denis Smith made the last of his 482 appearances, which had spanned over fourteen years since 1968, for his home town club. This proud Stokie was an exceptional player and servant to the club. Some players are "big time Charlies" who go missing in the lower profile games. Others love a starring role when the opposition is weak.

But Denis knew only one way to play - he gave it everything in every game. He made nearly 500 appearances for Stoke yet played every game as though it was his last. And it was an almost unique characteristic that, added to his fantastic ability to defend, made him one of the country's top centre-halves and a true Stoke legend.

Recognition and an Award

Argentina invaded the Falklands, leading to a war that was eventually won by British forces. Richard Attenborough's *Gandhi* was an epic masterpiece. The alien known as *ET* gave Spielberg another big hit.

Rambo kicked ass while his antithesis Boy George sang *"Do you really want to hurt me?"* And *The Young Ones* were fabulously anarchic.

Famous pottery designer Susie Cooper celebrated her 80th birthday with an exhibition of her work in London's Regent Street.

And our City Museum in Hanley won the 'Museum of the Year' Award.

1982/83 Season: Division 1

Doc Martins boots & slogans on T shirts

A farmer buys a field

My brother Steve says he once heard a manager on the radio being asked to evaluate the new player he'd just brought in on a free transfer. "He's good for nothing", was his reply. It still triggers Steve off to this day.

But there was no such ambiguous hilarity about George Berry's free transfer from Wolves to Stoke. George, who became a bit of a cult figure with Stoke fans, turned out to be very good for nothing and went on to hold down a regular place in our defence for some years.

Another popular player was Welsh international Mickey Thomas who also joined pre-season. Though small, Mickey was a tough, classy and creative left-sided midfielder who chipped in with his fair share of goals.

And future England winger Mark Chamberlain, brought in from the Vale, proved to be a fantastic acquisition who took the spot on the right of midfield.

Richie Barker had, to his credit, spent wisely and put together a midfield of Chamberlain, Bracewell, McIlroy and Thomas that had pace, creativity and class.

It was a pity that we'd let forwards Chapman, Crooks and Heath leave the club because they would've revelled in playing in front of this lot.

The League Campaign

Another opening day win over Arsenal, and that's for the second successive year. Then we lost 1-0 at Man City, won 4-1 at Birmingham, lost at home 3-0 to the Baggies, but beat Swansea 4-1 and won 3-2 at Ipswich. And those results were just a bit of a see-saw ride to prepare us for what came next.

You get these games occasionally, coming out of the blue, just when you're not expecting them. A nice, warm late-summer afternoon and 18,475 people turn up at the Victoria Ground to see Stoke v Luton.

We'd just scored 7 goals in the process of winning our last two games and they'd won their last match 5-0, so we could reasonably expect to see some decent football and a few goals from two good sides, both in form.

Ooh, Georgie Berry...

George proved again that he was very good for nothing and put us 1-0 in front with one of his rare goals. Sky TV's Paul Walsh scored a cracking equaliser from 25 yards before goal-machine George popped up again to make it 2-1.

Then Foxy got himself sent off and Brian Stein made it 2-2, and all this was before half-time. Early in the second half Paul Bracewell put us 3-2 in the lead, but Luton came back against 10 men Stoke, scored twice and nosed in front at 4-3.

Then Brendan made it 4-4 before Luton were awarded a last-gasp penalty.

Whether 18,000 Stoke fans unconsciously effected telekinesis I don't know, but the ball hit the post, bounced back out and judging from the celebrations you'd have thought we'd won the European Cup. It finished 4-4 and the goals are on youtube. Have a look.

Then we lost six of our next eight games. But things settled down in the second half of the season as we won eight matches (including those against Man United and Man City) drew six and lost only seven.

Overall, it was an entertaining season. We played some of our best football for a while and this was reflected in the average gate creeping up to nearly 17,000.

We finished a respectable 13th, scoring 47 against 64, but it was clear that we hadn't replaced the goalscoring talents of Chapman and Crooks as Mickey Thomas's eleven goals from midfield saw him come in as top scorer. And we'd averaged less than a goal per game since January.

Tuesday: Went to shops for bread and milk. Invaded Poland.

The so-called "Hitler diaries" were revealed to be a hoax. *The Return of the Jedi* was top film at the box office. And Eddie Murphy, Dan Aykroyd and Jamie Lee Curtis starred in *Trading Places*.

The Breakfast Show started on the BBC. Michael Jackson's *Billie Jean*, The Police with *Every Breath You Take* and Culture Club's *Karma Chameleon* topped the singles charts.

The Lombard RAC Rally was held at Trentham Gardens. And a Staffordshire farmer bought a field which, 26 years later, was found to contain the Saxon Hoard of gold.

1983/84 Season: Division 1

Shiny tracksuits & Rubik's Cube

Signal Radio goes on air

"Pay attention, chaps", as the modern football coach might now say while pointing to a flip chart with his swagger stick. "The goal is here, and the enemy – sorry, I mean the opposition's defence – is here, here and here." And this season Stoke was amongst the clubs incorporating the tactics for "Route One" football that were based on the theories of former Wing Commander Charles Reep.

The Wing Commander's analytical approach had been applied to football and it was concluded (I might be paraphrasing here) that the midfield was a bit of No Man's Land. Passing a football around could be very entertaining at times, but what won games were goals. And goals were scored usually when a team got the ball into the opposition's penalty box. This was known as a "Position Of Maximum Opportunity" (POMO).

And the more times they POMO'd, the more likely they were to score. So don't worry about too much about the midfield; let the opposition have it; they won't score many from there. Just win the ball, pump it up into the opposition's box and statistics will do the rest –especially if you've got a couple of big guys up front.

It worked for clubs like Wimbledon, who not only went up through the leagues but won the FA Cup as well. And with four international midfielders in our team, we tried some of it too.

67

Paul Bracewell out: Robbie James in

We lost five of our first six games, including a 5-0 drubbing at Ipswich, who didn't play Route One, and 4-0 at Watford, who did. We also failed to score in any of these five defeats. Then we won only one of our next ten games and the crowd levels at the Victoria Ground dropped alarmingly.

So the Board sacked Richie and installed former Potter's full-back Bill Asprey as manager.

But things were slow to improve. Bill won only one of his first eight games in charge and these included us being on the wrong end of a 6-0 hammering at QPR. And the crowd for our 1-1 home draw to Everton was 8,435. We had won only 3 of our first 24 games of the season, failing to score in eleven of them, and looked certainties for relegation. Then Bill brought 33 year-old Alan Hudson back to Stoke.

Huddy's back!

The Potteries started buzzing again because one of its heroes was back at Stoke. Although well past his best, the amazing thing about Alan Hudson was that he could still dominate a top football match with two of the slower legs and one of the quickest brains in the game.

His first game back was against his former club Arsenal at the Vic. Even the guys in the Butler Street Stand had painted a big banner saying "LOOK OUT! – HUDDY'S BACK!".

And, boy, was he back. We'd won only once in our last 16 games, but we won this one as Huddy strolled around the pitch and kept the ball like it belonged to him.

That was our fourth win in 25 games: only 17 left to save ourselves from relegation.

But we did it. Alan Hudson had the same season-changing impact as he'd had a decade earlier, and as Stan had had a decade before that.

We won another nine and drew three of our final 17 games, avoiding relegation on the last day of the season with a 4-0 win over Wolves, Paul Maguire scoring all four.

With that last day flurry, Maguire had finished as top scorer with 9, young Ian Painter got 8, Mark Chamberlain 7 and Robbie James bagged 6 from central midfield. Huddy didn't score: didn't need to.

Almost an irrelevance, but we went out of the League Cup in Round 4 and the FA Cup in Round 3.

Puppets scare rich and famous

The Miners went on strike warning that we were closing pits with a thousand years' worth of coal still underground.

Tommy Cooper died of a heart attack on stage. *Ghostbusters* was one of the big family films and the brilliant *Amadeus* did well at the Academy Awards.

Phil Collins sang *Against All Odds*. Politicians and celebrities ducked for cover as *Spitting Image* took to the small screen.

There was a roller-skates revival and having a filofax became the craze for those who couldn't skate.

And the Roebuck Centre opened in Newcastle.

1984/85 Season: Division 1

Wolstanton Colliery closes

When Captain Blackadder was asked what he thought about Baldrick's war poem he offered the opinion that "It started badly; it tailed off a little in the middle, and the less said about the end the better".

A useful quote, that. One which you can detach from its original context and use for anything that's irritatingly bad, chronically hopeless, excruciatingly painful or just plain unbearably bloody awful – like much of this season.

But I suppose that if I was making a pitch for the Understatement Of The Millennium I'd say it's seasons like this that make you appreciate the good times.

Or make you take up fishing.

It started badly

We won only one of our first twenty games. We beat Sheffield Wednesday 2-1 with goals from Sammy Mac and Phil Heath. And Wednesday were having a good season; they went on to finish 8th in the table.

It tailed off a little in the middle

But only after we beat Manchester United 2-1 at the Vic on Boxing Day! Carl Saunder and Ian Painter with a penalty got the goals. *It was the first game we'd won in four months.* United went on to finish 4th in the table.

And the less said about the end the better

Then the only game we won in the second half of the season was when we beat Arsenal 2-0 at the Vic. We did it with a rare goal from centre-back Paul Dyson and another Ian Painter penalty. Arsenal finished in 7th place in the table.

We then lost our next two games, 5-0 at Man United and 4-0 at home to Luton.

Then Bill Asprey, who'd done a fantastic job in keeping us up last year, was sacked.

Coach Tony Lacey was subsequently appointed as caretaker manager for the last eight games and lost them all. But, although it's the managers who carry the can for results, the responsibility for a season like this must be shared by all involved.

A reflection of how bad things had become around the club was the fact that our run of eleven consecutive defeats at the end of the season was the worst in our history to date.

The final countdown

We finished bottom with a (then) record low of 17 points. Amazingly, Norwich finished with 49 points and also got relegated with us.

We scored a total of 24 goals and failed to score at all in 25 games. And we conceded 91 goals.

Our average gate fell to 10,660, while only 4,597 turned up to see us lose 3-2 at home to Norwich.

Robbie James, Huddy and Peter Fox all struggled with injuries this season and only made fleeting appearances. And, for me, it was Sammy Mac who stood out as the class act.

It would be 23 long years before we returned to the top flight. And if you're just dragging yourself back up off your knees, the Cup performances weren't any improvement on the league.

We went out of the League Cup in Round Two to Rotherham and out of the FA Cup in Round Three to Luton.

Pound notes and coal

The miners' strike ended and Wolstanton colliery closed.

Chancellor Nigel Lawson announced that pound notes would be replaced with coins.

There were two football disasters, at the Bradford Stadium and the Heysel Stadium, within three weeks of each other.

Torvill & Dean won the Ice Dance gold medal and seventeen year old Boris Becker won Wimbledon.

Dennis Taylor came from 8-0 down to beat Steve Davis with the last shot of the Snooker World Championship and then wagged his finger at the audience.

Eastenders made its TV debut, as did Jeremy Brett in *The Casebook of Sherlock Holmes*.

Dire Straits sang *Money for Nothing* and Billy Oceon told us what the tough do *When The Going Gets Tough*.

And Michael J Fox went *Back To The Future*.

1985/86 Season: Division 2

National Garden Festival opens in Etruria

Everything we see is in the past. Everything. That's because the light reflected from whatever object it is we're looking at takes time to travel to our eyes. Then our brains have to process the information to make sense of the image.

Things that are a very long way off, such as our moon and sun, are seen by us as they were a few minutes earlier. It takes that long for the light which left their surface to reach our eyes. And the stars we see on a clear night might not, for all I know, be there any longer as the light we're seeing was reflected from their surfaces thousands of years ago.

And all this means, to my unscientific brain, that somewhere out there in space are light images of everything that's ever happened on our planet. And any Stoke supporting scientists who found a way of capturing those images could see all the games from past seasons as though they were recorded on DVD. But there isn't much from last season they'd want to watch again.

But there was more worth watching this season.

Mick Mills

Former Ipswich and England left-back Mick Mills had been appointed pre-season as player/manager. He came with over forty England caps to his name, a bushy moustache and a reputation for captaining "unfashionable" Ipswich in the period when they won a couple of Cups and were twice runners-up in the League.

The Board clearly hoped that in his first management job Mick could do something similar with "unfashionable" Stoke.

But many Stoke fans were disillusioned by last season and our average gate dropped to 8,228, the lowest, other than in wartime, for nearly eighty years.

Mick tried his best, there's no denying that. He made 31 appearances at left-back and led by example, but his squad was lacking in quality.

Mark Chamberlain

Mark Chamberlain played in the first seven games of the season, scoring 3 goals, before moving back to the First Division with Sheffield Wednesday. His final game for Stoke was a 1-1 draw played in front of a crowd of 4,255 at Middlesbrough.

The Great Huddy exits the stage

And Huddy's legs wouldn't let him do it anymore. He made only six appearances at the beginning of the season before hanging up his boots.

The man who had been a colossus in his first spell, and who had returned to help save us from relegation, played his final game in a Stoke shirt at the Victoria Ground in front of a crowd of 7,130 in a 0-0 draw against Crystal Palace.

Graham Shaw and Neil Adams

With the season progressing in a very average sort of way – we'd only won 2 of our first 14 games – Mick decided to give young lads Graham Shaw and Neil Adams a run in the side.

Both seemed at first glance to be small and slightly built. But they were tough lads who could hold their own.

Neil was a clever winger who made 31 appearances and chipped in with four goals.

And Shawry showed what he was capable of in a striker's role when he latched on to the ball just inside Huddersfield's half. He took off towards the Stoke End goal, waltzed past a couple of defenders and planted the ball in the net.

Great goal, but it almost makes you wonder whether starting like that is a blessing or a curse. It can really raise expectations and give a player a lot to live up to.

The other highlights of the season were us beating Leeds 6-2 and watching striker Keith Bertschin celebrating like he'd won a 'Pies for Life' competition each time he scored one of his 21 League and Cup goals.

Keith was easily our top scorer in a season when we finished 10th, scoring 48 goals against 50.

An even better theatre-in-the-round

Harrison Ford had a hit with *Witness,* as did Paul Hogan with *Crocodile Dundee.* And Tom Cruise was *Top Gun.*

Diana Ross sang *Chain Reaction* and Bon Jovi was *Living on a Prayer*. And *'Allo 'Allo'* was our favourite TV show.

The Moat House Hotel opened on the Festival site as the New Vic Theatre moved to its present site in Hartshill.

1986/87 Season Division 2

The Potteries Way ring-road built in Hanley

Play-offs were introduced this season to the Football League to spice up the promotion and relegation issues. But they were in a different format in 86/87 than the one we're used to in the 2010/11 season.

The format originally introduced in 86/87 was that the three clubs (Leicester, Manchester City and Aston Villa) who finished at the bottom of the First Division (equivalent to the modern day Premier League) were definitely relegated.

But the club finishing 4th from the bottom (in this case Charlton) had to scrap it out in the play-offs with those finishing 3rd, 4th & 5th in the Second Division (Oldham, Leeds and Ipswich).

The result was a Charlton v Leeds final. Charlton won and stayed in the Premier League.

And everybody sucked in air through their teeth and waited for the pedantic to say "what a waste of time that'd been, then".

Lee Dixon

Player/manager Mick Mills was in charge for his second full season. He made three appearances as a player at the start of the season and another three at the end. Other than that, he hung up his boots and focussed on management.

He had a good eye for a signing, did Mick.

During pre-season he'd signed a young right-back from Bury named Lee Dixon for a modest fee of £40K. That's not a lot to get excited about on the face of it, except that Lee turned out to be possibly the best right-back we've had at Stoke.

Lee was a terrific defender and had phenomenal energy which allowed him to overlap on the right in such a way that it seemed we'd got an extra player on that flank.

And Steve Bould, developing all the time as a top class defender, was moved inside from right-back to centre-back.

Mick also brought in his ex-Ipswich team mate Brian Talbot to bolster our midfield, Simon Stainrod to play up front and a young local lad Chris Maskery made a handful of appearances in central midfield.

Highlights & Lowlights

Although we missed the play-offs by 6 points there were plenty of highlights in what was quite an entertaining season.

We'd scored more goals (63) than conceded (53) and average crowds crept up to nearly 10K.

Home form wasn't bad with wins of 7-2 over Leeds, 5-2 over Sheffield United and 5-1 over Grimsby. There were also away wins of 4-0 at Hull and 4-1 at Bradford.

And our goal fests included hat-tricks for Keith Bertschin, Carl Saunders and Nicky Morgan.

Saunders finished the season as top scorer with 19 League & Cup goals, Morgan with 12 and Bertschin with 8.

But for a team that played some cracking football this season we had a few uncharacteristic reverses. We lost 3-1 at Sheffield United, 4-1 at West Brom and again 4-1 at Shrewsbury.

The League & FA Cups

We did okay this season, narrowly losing by 1-0 to Liverpool at their place in an FA Cup 3rd Round replay.

And we knocked Gillingham and Norwich out of the League Cup before we got knocked out ourselves at Arsenal.

Chernobyl and Challenger

Challenger space shuttle exploded killing seven astronauts and the Russians experienced nuclear disaster at Chernobyl.

Bands with place names topped the charts. Berlin sang *Take My Breath Away*, Europe sang *The Final Countdown* and Stokie Slash released *Sweet Child of Mine* with Guns n Roses.

Both Sean Connery and Kevin Costner put in great performances in *The Untouchables,* while *Three Men and a Baby* was the year's top box-office film.

On Christmas Day 1986 over thirty million viewers watched *Eastenders*.

The National Garden Festival closed in Etruria after being a great success. Plans were in place to re-develop the site as a huge business and leisure complex.

And the Spitfire was moved to the inside of our City museum.

<u>1987/88 Season: Division 2</u>

Potteries Shopping Centre opens in Hanley

When it comes to spending your Saturday afternoons either shopping or watching Stoke there's usually no contest. But our club now had some serious competition in Hanley.

Many Stoke fans were still disillusioned by the fact that five of our best young players had been allowed to leave in recent seasons and two more followed them out of the door this time round. And that's not a policy for taking the club to the Promised Land.

We all know that forecasting anything can leave you with egg on your face. But just as it's a safe bet most days that tomorrow's weather won't differ greatly from today's, it was a fair bet this season that a lot of Stokies would be found in the new Potteries Shopping Centre in Hanley rather than at the Victoria Ground.

So the average gate remained stubbornly below 10,000; a clear indication that many fans thought the club wasn't on track to get out of this Division. As fans we always hope the club will out-perform expectations, but realistically this was a season more about damage-limitation than progression.

The League Campaign

Mick would've just been settling into his seat in the Away dugout at St Andrews when we went behind after 45 seconds of our opening game of the season. We didn't get back into the game and lost 2-0 to Birmingham.

We were inconsistent and lacking punch at times, and it showed in the fact that we failed to score in 8 of our first 16 games. But then, and all credit to Mick and the players, we found some form and went on a decent run.

During the next 21 games (half a season's worth of football) we won eleven, drew four and lost only six. And we scored more than twice the number of goals (34) than the 16 we managed in the other half of the season.

There were good wins over West Brom, Bradford, Reading and Birmingham at our place, but the Stoke lads mustn't have liked the thin air around the Pennines as we were hammered 5-1 at Oldham and 5-2 at Barnsley.

Overall, though, it was another middling season lacking in promise. We finished 11th in the table, scoring 50 against 57, with Phil Heath finishing as top scorer with eight and Graham Shaw coming in second with six.

Lee Dixon & Steve Bould

In recent years the club had allowed Crooks, Chapman, Heath, Bracewell and Chamberlain to leave. And this season Lee Dixon was sold to Arsenal for £400K, with Steve Bould joining him for £390K just four months later.

That's a total of seven top young players allowed to leave in a few years. The fans weren't happy about our best players leaving, while the Board claimed they had no choice but to sell as gates were low.

It's a situation that raises the old dilemma of where a football club lies on the spectrum between being a business and a community-supported institution.

Few other businesses would be able to draw on such unconditional loyalty of thousands of customers. That said, a professional football club has to run as a business and balance the books.

One thing is for sure, though, the more that money dominates the professional game, the more difficult these questions are to resolve – not only for Stoke, but for all clubs.

Talking of how money has come to dominate the game, Chelsea were relegated to the Second Division in 1987/88.

Twenty years later, with a billionaire owner in place, there's less chance of Chelsea facing relegation than non-league Luton Town returning to the mid-table finish they had in the First Division in 1987/88.

Rain Man and Weather Man

BBC weatherman Michael Fish dismissed a claim that a hurricane was on the way just before the worst winds in centuries hit Britain and Sevenoaks in Kent lost six of the original seven oak trees that gave the town its name.

Tom Cruise exploited Dustin Hoffman's unusual talents in *Rain Man,* while Bruce Willis and Alan Rickman were classic opponents in *Die Hard*.

Meanwhile, in deepest space, a clever assortment of humans and non-humans had fun in *Red Dwarf*.

And Robbie Williams was in an amateur production of *Fiddler on the Roof* at the Theatre Royal.

1988/89 Season: Division 2

First ever Oatcake fanzine:

Stoke v Swindon on 19-11-1988

In Waddo's day tickets for three sweepstake competitions were sold around the pits, pot banks and other work places. The massive £45,000 per week income generated by these sales, along with the increased gate revenue, helped him to bring a host of stars to Stoke.

Since then we've had Golden Goal tickets, Half Time Draw tickets and other money making schemes.

Football clubs have to raise money of course, there's no problem with that. It's an expensive business to run. And selling hats and scarves in the team colours, and replica kits, and so on, are all good marketing ideas.

But there was one match this season, our home game with Manchester City, when their fans stood wafting around big inflatable bananas and Stoke fans had bought inflatable pink panthers from the club shop to wave back at them.

These fads last about five minutes. And the "let's be fair to everyone" voice in my head says they're only a bit of fun.

But when I got my feet tangled up in one of these deflated toys that somebody had chucked on the floor I nearly went flying down the Boothen End steps. Then the grumpy old git voice in my head told him to bugger off and said it's five bloody minutes too long.

Peter Beagrie & Chris Kamara

Before Mick began his fourth season in charge he'd demonstrated his eye for a decent player again. He bolstered our midfield with the signing of combative Chris Kamara and classy winger Peter Beagrie.

Chris was one of those ultra-passionate types who could whip up the supporters into a frenzy even if he was playing on Wolstanton Marsh. And Peter would twist and turn defenders inside out before scoring and doing that gymnastic back-flip thing that's since become quite common.

The League Campaign

Division Two was expanding as the First Division was getting smaller, so we played a total of 46 League games (more than any previous season). But we were slow off the mark, failing to score in nine and winning only seven of our first 21 games. We had a good 4-0 win over Hull, but we'd been beaten by the same score by Plymouth and Leeds. And against West Brom we were even worse, losing 6-0.

Then Mick added full-back John Butler and striker Dave Bamber to the squad. They both made their debuts on Boxing Day, obviously signing for us so they could see thousands of inflated toys dotted around the stadium. Bamber scored and we won 3-1.

We then hit a patch of good form as that was the first of seven wins in the next eleven games.

But for some reason our form then really fell away and a 1-0 win over Bournemouth was our only victory in our last fourteen games. And our final game of the season was a home draw with Brighton in front of a crowd of only 5,841.

Overall, it was another uninspiring season and we finished thirteenth, scoring 57 against 72. Peter Beagrie's eight goals meant he finished easily as our top scorer. And the average gate stubbornly remained under 10,000.

The Cups

There wasn't even the solace of a good Cup run.

We went out of the League Cup to Leyton Orient after a Second Round replay.

And although we scraped past Crystal Palace 1-0 in the 3rd Round of the FA Cup, we went out in Round 4 to Barnsley following another replay.

And a Barnsley scorer caught Beagrie Fever and copied his somersault. In truth, he might have even done it a bit better.

Cash in the attic

Sky Television first went on air in the UK. And Frank Bruno lost to Mike Tyson in a World Heavyweight contest.

The Inland Revenue shared top billing with Ken Dodd at Liverpool Crown Court. Suit cases containing £335,000 in notes had been found in his attic.

The jury found Doddy guilty of being very funny, but not guilty of anything else.

And Waterworld opened on the Festival site in Etruria.

1989/90 Season: Division 2

Gaumont cinema in Piccadilly closes

Pavlov's dogs salivated at the sound of a bell because that's when they knew they were about to be fed. It's what's called a "conditioned response". It's like that queasy feeling you get when what is laughingly called "reality TV" comes on the telly. Or that sense of doom some of us had at the start of this season when so much was made of our quest for promotion.

This is Stoke we're on about and you just knew it was like tempting fate, kicking dirt all over The Path of Good Intentions, coming face to face with Optimism, head-butting him on the bridge of the nose and kneeing him in the groin.

We got relegated. We went down to the Third Division for only the second time in our history, the last being 1926/27.

Ian Cranson & Wayne Biggins

Looking back, Mick had a real talent in spotting players. He'd already brought in Lee Dixon and Peter Beagrie; both top signings.

He'd converted Steve Bould from a full-back to a first class centre-back. And John Butler and Chris Kamara had both been good value.

And now Mick used the money at his disposal to bring in centre-back Ian Cranson and striker Wayne Biggins; terrific signings that would become crowd favourites. But we just couldn't find a consistent winning formula.

The League Campaign

We won only one of our first sixteen games of the season. And we lost seven of them - including a 6-0 defeat at Swindon - which was Mick's last game in charge before he was sacked. And Peter Beagrie had been allowed to leave for First Division Everton for a fee of £750K.

Alan Ball

Another ex-England international, Alan Ball, was then brought in as manager. Bally soon got cracking bringing in his own men, including defenders Lee Sandford and big Noel Blake from Portsmouth where Alan had previously been manager. Striker Tony Ellis came in to partner Wayne Biggins. Dave Kevan came into midfield. And Mickey Thomas was brought back for the last two months of the season.

But the formula for a winning team was still missing. It must've been put in a drawer and forgotten about, or lost down the back of the sofa, or something.

Of the thirty league games that Alan was in charge this season we won five and failed to score in sixteen of them.

Record signing Ian Cranson made only 11 appearances at the beginning of the season then missed the rest of the campaign through injury. If he'd stayed fit there's little doubt he would've improved our defensive record, but our main problem stemmed from the fact the team just couldn't score enough goals.

We finished bottom of the league with 37 points, scoring only 35 goals and conceding 63.

Everybody associated with the club was, to put it mildly, unhappy. And it's times like these, when things have gone wrong, that people start playing the blame game.

Some blamed the manager, although for his part Alan reckoned - probably with some justification - that the responsibility for Stoke's demise couldn't all be laid at his door.

So everybody seemed to have some responsibility; although, as far as I know, nobody blamed the government.

The Cups

We went out of the League Cup in Round 2 and out of the FA Cup in Round 3. Enough said.

More satellite dishes

Sky Sports channel first came on air.

Kevin Costner did *Dances With Wolves*. Pavarotti's *Nessun Dorma* (none shall sleep) topped the charts because of its success as a World Cup theme.

Jeremy Paxman made his debut on *Newsnight*.

Victor Meldrew's famous catch-phrase caught on from *One Foot in the Grave*.

The Simpsons made its debut and became one of the best things to come on TV for twenty years.

Florence colliery closed and the Regent Theatre in Hanley became a Listed Building.

1990/91 Season: Division 3

Phil Taylor wins his first

World Darts Championship

Any Stoke fan that was supporting the club around this time might still be in therapy twenty years later. Last season had ended with a disastrous relegation. And this season we were still on the slide like a novice on the Piste.

Alan Ball had brought in central midfielder Mick Kennedy, another of his ex Pompey players to join up again with Lee Sandford and Noel Blake.

We won our opening two games and Kennedy scored in both. A good start; but after that it all went downhill like a runaway HGV on Kidsgrove bank.

We were up against supposedly inferior opposition in this lower Division but we managed only five wins in Alan's next 27 games in charge.

And the mood amongst the fans (those I knew, anyway) through much of the season was worse than it usually is in those argumentative soaps on the telly.

Then, on 23rd February '91, Bally resigned after the team's latest catastrophic defeat by 4-0 at Wigan.

"Budgie"

Peter Coates had taken over the chairmanship of the Board last season and now turned to Alan's assistant, Graham

Paddon to manage the club for the remaining 18 games of this season. Graham had been nicknamed "Budgie" in his days as a player at Norwich due to his likeness to Adam Faith who played a TV private detective of that name.

The Canaries seem to have this thing about bird names.

Budgie didn't get off to the best of starts. We lost 3-1 at the Victoria Ground to Bournemouth in his first match. But we had a good win of 4-0 at Brentford and we beat Mansfield 3-1 at the Vic. There were four other narrow wins, but Budgie lost 9 and drew 3 of the remaining games where he was in charge.

The few high points of the season were Mickey Thomas making 32 appearances and scoring 7 goals. Tony Ellis scored 9 goals, while Wayne Biggins came in as top scorer with 12.

Possibly the brightest spot was Carl Beeston holding down a regular place in midfield.

Incredibly, the average gates for last season, when we were relegated, and this season in the Third Division, were both higher than in the previous four seasons in a higher Division.

But our finishing place of 14th in Division 3 this season marked the lowest point in the club's history.

Where now?

Stoke had had three managers in the last 18 months yet we'd plunged to our worst place ever. We had some very good players on the books such as Fox, Butler, Sandford, Cranson, Beeston and Biggins, yet the team didn't look greater than the sum of the parts.

It didn't seem like the Board had the means to make a major investment and the fans were disillusioned.

We needed a manager who could motivate the players, get them to defend as a unit and give them belief and a winning mentality. Somebody who could work within the constraints set by the Board. Somebody who could win back some of the lost fans and get them behind the team.

Then Peter Coates pulled off a master stroke by bringing in a little bloke, with a Scottish accent and a curly fringe.

The Web

The World Wide Web was launched and changed all our lives.

The Silence of the Lambs cleaned up at the Oscars and *Thelma & Louise* made an impression on Brad Pitt.

The writer, social commentator and former hippy PJ O'Rourke released the excellent *Parliament of Whores*.

Oliver Reed was drunk on Michael Aspel's chat show. And a turquoise-track-suited David Icke appeared on the Wogan show.

The first episode of *Have I got News For You* was broadcast and became an enduring hit.

The statue of war hero Jack Baskeyfield, who had been awarded the Victoria Cross, was erected at the Festival Park.

Phil Taylor began a long sequence of winning Darts championships and Robbie Williams became the youngest member of Take That.

1991/92 Season: Division 3

Jollees cabaret club closes

"I'm gobsmacked he's agreed to come" was my brother Big Al's response to the news that Lou Macari had been appointed pre-season as Stoke's new manager.

He wasn't the only one. Lou had a fine track record in management. He'd got Swindon promoted twice, had done a good job at West Ham and his last club, Birmingham City, had even offered him a new three-year contract. And worth mentioning because it's not often the case that fans want the manager to stay, but in Lou's case at Birmingham, they did.

But the manager's job at Celtic was vacant at the time and it seemed like that might be Lou's preferred destination. And while he was pondering Celtic, Stoke reportedly made an approach for up-and-coming manager Harry Redknapp at Bournemouth but, for whatever reason, he stayed put.

The upshot of it all was that Lou didn't get the Celtic job and it was high-fives all round when he accepted our offer.

Start with a stumble

Aussie 'keeper Jason Kearton had been brought in and replaced Peter Fox in goal, but we still lost our first game of the season 1-0 away to Bradford.

On the face of it nothing much had changed. But then Lou was able to bring in some key players and put his own stamp on our style of play.

Vince Overson

Commanding centre-back Vince Overson followed Lou into the club from Birmingham. Vince partnered fit-again Ian Cranson in the heart of the defence with John Butler and Lee Sandford at full-back.

And after a couple of months Ronnie Sinclair joined Stoke and took over in goal. Ronnie looked small for a 'keeper, but he'd got "safe hands", and with Vince and Cranny in front of him that's all he needed.

Mark Stein

The team still needed more of a cutting edge and to everybody's surprise a little bloke with chunky legs was brought in from Oxford reserves.

Mark Stein came initially on loan for five games and failed to score in any of them. Then Lou shelled out £100K to bring him back to Stoke on a permanent basis.

It's an unjust law of human nature that nobody comments when you get things right but they keep dragging it up if you get the slightest thing wrong, like forgetting to turn up for a job interview or your wedding. I might have mentioned during his loan period that I thought Mark Stein wasn't the answer to our goal scoring problems and Al still can't let it go all these years later.

Anyway, everything about the team suddenly clicked. And Steino not only scored 17 goals in his next 33 appearances, but also proved to be the perfect partner for Wayne (Bertie) Biggins who finished the season as top scorer with 22.

Steve Foley had come in for the second half of the season to add a bit of graft and creativity to midfield, and winger Kevin "Rooster" Russell showed his qualities when he made five appearances on loan.

But for some poor results in the run-in we could've got automatic promotion. Unfortunately, we finished 4th with 77 points, scoring 69 against 49, and ended up losing to Stockport in the play-offs.

But we did win our first trophy in twenty years, the Autoglass, and gained some revenge on Stockport by beating them 1-0 at Wembley with a great goal by the little bloke who, I'm happy to say, proved me wrong.

And ignoring the fact that we went out of the First Round of the FA Cup to Telford, we did well in the Cup competitions this season. Liverpool only scraped past us 3-2 in a replay after our heroic draw at Anfield.

Premier League launched

Euro Disney opened in Paris. Sharon Stone made Michael Douglas sweat in *Basic Instinct*. Tom Cruise and Jack Nicholson were protagonists in *A Few Good Men* and Daniel Day-Lewis was *The Last of the Mohicans*.

The top TV show was *Men Behaving Badly*.

The government ordered construction of the A50 Blythe Bridge to Queensway trunk road.

And the Premier League was created when this season ended.

1992/93 Season: Division 2

North Staffs Poly becomes Staffordshire University

The National lottery hadn't been launched yet, so it was the football pools we were checking every Saturday while dreaming of the freedoms money can bring.

It doesn't happen to many, but everybody in football felt like they'd won the pools when twenty-two clubs had broken away from the Football League and formed the Premier League.

For starters, this new elite would keep for themselves most of the many millions of pounds that would flow in from the pay-per-view television channels.

And everybody else gets promoted to a higher Division.

The Second Division becomes the First Division, and so on. We're now in Division 2. It's all win-win.

Or is it? The first Premier League included in their number clubs like Wimbledon and Oldham. And Norwich, QPR and Sheffield Wednesday all finished above Chelsea, Arsenal, Spurs and Man City this season.

But the big clubs knew what they were doing. Thirteen of the original 22 were in lower leagues within a few years.

Nigel Gleghorn

Lou brought in another of his former Birmingham players, classy midfield play-maker Nigel Gleghorn. And Rooster returned permanently along with striker Dave Regis.

And, surprisingly, Wayne Biggins was allowed to move to Barnsley. Losing Bertie was a real blow as he stood out at this level, but overall the squad looked strong.

The League campaign – Promotion!

When we won only one of our first seven games there was little to suggest how the rest of the season would unfold. But we went on to win 26, draw 8 and lose only 5 of our remaining 39 games.

And we ended up being promoted as Champions with 93 points.

It all really started with a pulsating 4-3 win over West Brom at the Victoria Ground. It was the first of four games this season in which we scored four goals.

In fact, goals weren't a problem – at either end of the pitch. We scored a total of 73 and conceded a miserly 34 in 46 games, due in a small degree to celebrity loan signing Bruce Grobelaar turning out in goal for us in four games when our regulars were injured.

Mark Stein finished out-and-out top scorer with 26, and the rest were shared out amongst the team. Ever-present Nigel Gleghorn got 7 (including the crucial winner against Plymouth that clinched promotion),

Steve Foley also got 7, Dave Regis and Graham Shaw bagged 5 each and even the defenders chipped in with their share.

And the average gate of 16,589 was our highest for ten years.

The Cups

We went out of the FA Cup to the Vale in the First Round and the League Cup to Cambridge. Enough said.

The evolution of football

We were the best footballing side in the Division this season, but I doubt we would've finished as champions without Lou's emphasis on physical fitness, teamwork and pure hard graft.

Tony Waddington's artists had graced football pitches with their class, but the game had since become increasingly organised and now greater importance was being placed on the aspect of strength and fitness.

Although we hadn't (yet) got a team of six-foot-plus giants, Lou's teams were able to leave many opposing sides gasping after 70 minutes. And that gave our players a huge advantage.

Splits

The Czechoslovakians voted to split into the Czech Republic and Slovakia. And there was another split when the Church of England voted to allow women priests. DNA fingerprinting was invented.

Kevin Costner was *The Bodyguard* and *Jurassic Park* was the big family film.

The top TV shows were *Between the Lines, Gladiators and The Simpsons* was going from strength to strength.

And there was a threat to 1400 jobs at Trentham Super-pit.

1993/94 Season

Satellite imaging shows the Potteries is sinking

Lemmings don't throw themselves off cliffs; not according to Wiki anyway. It's a common misconception; a myth.

But it's probably the kind of analogy the media were using to describe Stoke fans when, only twelve games into the season, Lou left us to take the manager's job at Celtic and Mark Stein was transferred to Chelsea for £1.6M in the same week.

Lou's managerial style had proved popular with the fans and Steino's goal-scoring record, 29 League and Cup goals last season and already 8 goals in 12 League games this season, meant that both men would be a huge loss to the club.

But an uninformed observer might've wondered what all the fuss was about. Chic Bates had taken over as caretaker manager for the next three games and won them all, including a 5-4 win over Barnsley at the Victoria Ground.

Joe Jordan

Then former Scotland and Man United striker Joe Jordan took over as manager for the rest of the season and got off to a good start by winning his first game, a 1-0 home win over Leicester in front of the TV cameras and a passionate Stoke crowd.

It seemed everybody was pulling together to cope with the losses we'd suffered.

But Joe struggled to sustain the momentum and we only won ten of the remaining thirty matches this season, with us failing to score in twelve of them.

Orlygsson, Carruthers and Prudhoe

Although these were three players Lou had brought in pre-season, they played most of their games this season under Joe.

Toddy was the first Icelander to play for Stoke and none of us at the time, probably including him, had any idea of the impact his signing for us would eventually have on both Stoke and Iceland.

Martin Carruthers was a young, pacey striker drafted in from Villa. And Mark Prudhoe was a Russ Abbott look-alike goalkeeper who, thankfully, didn't play like his doppelganger.

And after going five games in March '94 without us scoring, Joe brought Wayne Biggins back to the club, along with midfielder Mickey Adams and winger Mark Walters.

All three made their home debuts in the 3-0 win over Bristol City, with Adams scoring twice and Bertie bagging a penalty.

The three of them made a difference, scoring nine goals between them in the end of season run-in.

Toddy Orlygsson and Dave Regis finished the season as joint top scorers with ten goals each.

And Mark Stein was second top scorer with eight even though he'd left the club before the end of October '93.

Bearing in mind that it was our first season back at a higher level we did okay with a mid-table 10th place finish on 67 points, scoring 57 goals and conceding 59.

But some fans had never really come to terms with Lou Macari leaving Stoke.

The Cup competitions

Steino was still with Stoke when his two terrific finishes past Peter Schmeichel (they're on youtube) helped us to beat Man United 2-1 in the first of a two-leg League Cup Round at Stoke. But we lost the second leg 2-0.

And although we needed a replay to get past non-league Bath City in the Third Round of the FA Cup, we then went out in the Fourth Round to Oldham Athletic.

Death of Tony Waddington

Russian troops left Poland. Stephen Hawking's *A Brief History of Time* topped the book charts. And Michael Douglas was *Falling Down* big-time.

New series *Cracker* and the *Cheers* spin-off *Frasier* were TV successes.

Did the earth move for you? Satellite images showed a large proportion of the Potteries had slowly sunk, due to mining subsidence, in recent years.

And Stoke fans everywhere mourned the death of Tony Waddington, unquestionably one of Stoke's greatest managers, on 21st January 1994.

1994/95 Season: Division 1

Trentham Super-pit closes

It's as well to brace yourself for bad news. When asked why he'd been seen begging from statues the Greek philosopher Diogenes replied: "I'm practising disappointment".

But, although I'm sure Joe Jordan hadn't been on his knees next to the statue of Perseus and Medusa at Trentham Gardens, as Stoke manager he must've known that disappointment usually came with the job.

So it probably didn't come as a big surprise to him when he parted company with the club after Stoke lost four of their first five games this season.

Paul Peschisolido and Carl Muggleton

Joe had made a couple of good signings pre-season. Goalkeeper Carl Muggleton had joined, initially on loan, and highly-rated Birmingham striker Paul Peschisolido was also brought in for £400K plus Dave Regis.

Asa Hartford

Asa was famous for having been a professional footballer despite having a hole in his heart. That's definitely the case, but whether the story of him getting his first name because his dad was a fan of the singer Asa Jolson is true, I've no idea.

And Asa demonstrated a big heart when took the reins for a few weeks after Joe's departure and did well, winning all three games for which he was our caretaker manager.

Lou's back

But the clamour among the fans was for Lou to return. The Board clearly agreed and Lou returned on 29th September '94. And it lasted nearly three years.

Kevin Keen and Keith Scott

Lou was allowed to splash some cash and he brought in right-midfield player Kevin Keen for £300K. He then spent a similar amount on tall striker Keith Scott.

Keeno, who became a bit of a cult figure with the Stoke fans, was a hard-working, creative player capable of changing a game by doing something a bit different.

Scotty came with a reputation for being a goal scorer but, for whatever reason, he wasn't prolific at Stoke because he only scored 3 in 25 appearances.

League form

Lou had steadied the ship for the time he was in charge this season. One of the trademarks of a Macari team was that it was hard to beat.

And, sure enough, of the 35 games for which he was in charge we lost only eight, won 13, but we drew too many (14) to make an impact on the table.

And so we finished eleventh place in the table, scoring 50 and conceding 53.

A big bonus was that Pesch looked a good player and he finished as top scorer with 15.

There was a feeling among the fans that with some substantial investment in quality players Lou was the man to get us promoted to the riches of the Premier League.

And hopes were raised temporarily when the media reported that a local insurance broker was interested in taking over the club and putting up funds for players, but it never got off the ground. If we were going to do it, then it looked like we'd have to do it the hard way.

The Cups

We went out of the FA Cup to Bristol City after a replay.

But we knocked Fulham out of the League Cup and we gave a good account of ourselves at Liverpool in the next Round, only to lose narrowly at 2-1.

Oh my God, it's like totally awesome!

Yahoo and Amazon were launched.

And text messaging (C U 2mora m8) was introduced.

The first National Lottery draw was live on TV.

D:Ream sang *Things Can Only Get Better*. Tom Hanks was brilliant again as Forrest *Gump*. And Keanu Reeves and Sandra Bullock had a hit with *Speed*.

American sitcoms such as *Friends* influenced the way in which the English language is spoken.

And the Gladstone Museum in Longton was taken over by the council.

1995/96 Season: Division 1

The Oatcake goes on-line

Festival site re-opens as a Retail Park

For want of a nail the shoe was lost
For want of a shoe the horse was lost
For want of a horse the rider was lost
For want of a rider the battle was lost
For want of a battle the kingdom was lost
And all for the want of a horseshoe nail
(Old English proverb)

Despite the initial optimism surrounding Lou's return we started this season with only 3 wins in the first 14 games and crowds briefly dropped below 10,000.

Icelandic defender Laurus Siggurdsson had joined pre-season and looked a good acquisition. Overall we were a decent side, but we weren't scoring enough. The mood around the club wasn't right and there was some unrest on the terraces and in the dressing room.

It's times like this when a club needs decisive leadership, and we got it in two forms.

There was a rallying cry from captain Vince Overson and Lou shuffled things around by moving a couple of players out of the club and bringing in striker Simon Sturridge and midfielder Ray Wallace to replace them.
And there was one other crucial bit of business.

Mike Sheron

Mike joined Stoke as part of the deal that took Keith Scott to Norwich. Some players just need a change of club for their quality to come out. And Mike only had to pull a Stoke shirt over his head to be transformed into a souped-up goal machine, scoring 15 in 22 games.

This goal-fest included him scoring in seven consecutive games, a feat never previously achieved by any Stoke player.

Simon Sturridge was no slouch either and in Pesch's absence through injury, the "SAS" (Sheron And Sturridge) partnership looked the business with Studger chalking up twelve goals for himself.

With three goalscorers in the side confidence had soared and the Stoke players began performing as a top team again.

The mood both on and off the pitch lifted and we went on a terrific run with 17 wins and 8 draws in our last 32 games.

Without spending a fortune – there wasn't a fortune to be spent – Lou had put together a team whose style of play looked to be on permanent fast-forward, and which could've well been heading for the Premier League.

But this level of sustained effort takes its toll and it was beyond the team to make up for their poor start to the season and clinch automatic promotion.

Instead we finished fourth in the table and had to settle for the play-offs.

For want of a battle the kingdom was lost

Just before the transfer window closed Stoke sold Paul Peschisolido, one of our three prized strikers. In contrast, Leicester, who we were to face in the play-offs, signed three players to strengthen their bid for promotion. And we not only failed to score against them in either leg of the play-off semi-finals, but also lost to a goal scored by one of their new signings.
Then Leicester's investment was returned several times over by the influx of television money following their promotion to the "kingdom" of the Premier League.

Nobody can say for certain that we would've won the play-offs and promotion had Peschisolido stayed. But some Stoke fans believed it could have been a case of:-

> For want of a battle the kingdom was lost
> And all for the want of a horseshoe nail.

Maybe: we'll never know.

Dominic Cork and RJ Mitchell

Ebay and Wikipedia were both launched. Tom Hanks starred in *Apollo 13*. Classic series *Fawlty Towers* and *Father Ted* were our favourite television shows and made us wonder how much they were based on reality. Boyzone topped the charts with *Love Me for a Reason*.

Stoke fan Dominic Cork made his debut for the England cricket team. And it was the centenary of RJ Mitchell, one of our city's most important sons.

1996/97 Season: Division 1

Our final season at the Victoria Ground

We'd taken an hour off work, crammed into one of the free mini-buses that'd been laid on, had a bumpy ride to the new site, looked at the "artist's impression" on a display board and done the "virtual tour" on the lap-tops.

Then we stood gawping into the hollowed-out basin of land in front of us. It didn't look big enough to contain a football stadium, seemed to be in the middle of nowhere, looked like it was going to be a plastic and concrete experience and getting to it on match days was going to be a nightmare.

But, after 118 years at the Victoria Ground, we'd got just this one season remaining before we left the oldest football stadium in the world for our new home.

And our last season at the Vic was a strange affair in many ways.

Vince Overson, Nigel Gleghorn, Lee Sandford, Graham Potter and Ian Clarkson all left the club pre-season and Lou brought in midfielder Richard Forsyth, and full-back Ally Pickering. Then midfielder Graham Kavanagh and winger Gerry McMahon joined for around half-a-million each; big fees for us.

But it was a 17 year old lad who broke into the team and who looked equally comfortable at either full-back position that grabbed our attention.

Andy Griffin

Although not a big youth, Andy had reportedly played a lot of rugby and looked like he could handle the physical side of the game. He was quick, tenacious in the tackle and had the kind of energy levels that meant he could overlap all day.

And what none of us could've known at the time, Andy's association with Stoke would be a long one and he would go on to have the distinction of signing for us at four different times throughout his career.

The League campaign

With three wins and two draws in our first five games we were off to a good start, but then key players Simon Sturridge and Ian Cranson suffered long-term injuries. Then Mark Stein came back on loan for a couple of months and we were well placed by Christmas.

But our form fell away after that and we only won six of our last twenty games, failing to score in ten of them, although we did sign-off from the Victoria Ground with home wins over the Vale and West Brom.

On the back of last season's fantastic effort, and the fact that this was our last season at the Vic, we were hoping for something special this time round. It would've been something to leave our old home with a promotion and start life in our new one in the Premier League, but there were too many changes in key personnel and injuries to critical players. So it was all a bit of an anti-climax.

In what was an unusually tight table we finished in 12th place with 64 points, only 5 points off a play-off position, scoring 51 goals and conceding 57. Mike Sheron showed that last season was no flash in the pan and easily finished as top scorer with 24 goals. And our average gate was a modest 12,751.

Lou Macari leaves the club

Chic Bates and Mike Pejic took charge of the team for the final home game on the grounds that Lou was pursuing a lawsuit through the courts against Celtic, his previous employer.

And In what seemed to be a somewhat bizarre situation to the fans, there was some confusion over whether Lou would eventually return to take over the managerial reins. In the event, he never did.

Dolly

Dolly the sheep was the first cloned animal. Film director Fred Zinnemann (*High Noon* and *The Day of the Jackal*) died. Will Smith and Jeff Goldblum's *Independence Day* was one of the big hit family films.

Over twenty-four million Christmas viewers watched *Only Fools and Horses*. Ali G conducted some hilarious interviews with unsuspecting victims. The building used as Cauldon College was fifty years old.

And with the number of Internet football sites growing, many Stoke fans would never have guessed how much of their time they'd now be spending on-line.

1997/98 Season: Division 1

Our first season at the Britannia Stadium

The Bosman Ruling that had come in 18 months earlier was now beginning to have a dramatic effect on transfer fees for those players running out of contract.

Sheron out, Thorne in

Stoke exploited this situation and signed top striker Peter Thorne for a paltry £300K, one of the best deals in our recent history. And ex England player Paul Stewart came in on a freebie to partner him in attack because Mike Sheron had moved to QPR for what was then a massive fee of £2.5M.

Our first League game in our new home was against Thorney's former club Swindon. It was preceded by some razmataz involving a Tom Jones look-alike with a duff microphone ("I saw...night....passed...window").

Then a ball was placed at the end of the penalty box, instead of the 6-yard box, for 82 year old Sir Stan to score the first ever goal at the stadium. But his kick fell short of the goal line and then we lost to Swindon.

"Men are nearly always willing to believe what they wish", said Julius Caesar and the superstitious thereafter knew exactly why the rest of the season was such a disaster.

But at least we liked the look of the Brit and the views from the stands were great, especially with a full house, even if we did spend the first half of the season working out the best route to get there.

Chic Bates

Chic had proved an able lieutenant to Lou and was now in charge of the team, but things weren't going well by mid-season. A rumour went round that there was a list of players the club allegedly wanted rid of. And in our next home game a seemingly demoralised Stoke side was humiliated 7-0 by Birmingham at the Brit.

There was pandemonium among some fans in the stadium. And this game marked a low point in a disastrous season which had started full of eager anticipation.

Then Chic was demoted back to his role as assistant manager.

Chris Kamara

Former Stoke midfield warrior Chris Kamara returned to the club as manager.

Andy Griffin was sold to Newcastle for a big fee and Chris brought in goalkeeper Neville Southall and striker Kyle Lightbourne to partner Peter Thorne.

It was obvious to any onlooker that Chris was giving it everything but, for whatever reason, it didn't work out and we won only one of the fourteen games for which he was in charge before being sacked.

The Board then turned to Alan Durban, temporarily without a club, to return as manager for the last few games and save us from what seemed the inevitable. But it wasn't to be and we ended up second bottom and relegated in our first season at the Britannia.

It wasn't the case that we'd been relegated easily: had results gone our way on the last day we could've stayed up.

But the management position had been unsettled throughout the season, with too many contrasting styles. And the squad had lost too much quality and just wasn't good enough.

After all the excitement of moving to a new stadium, the reality of relegation was a bitter pill to swallow.

Remember the rider having lost his horse for want of a horseshoe nail? Billy reckoned that if he'd been the rider he'd have happily swapped the horse this season for a couple of day passes for Alton Towers, just to take his mind off things.

Bear climbs mountain

Over two billion people worldwide watched Diana's funeral on TV and Elton had a big hit with a specially written *Candle in the Wind*.

Bear Grylls, at 23, became the youngest British person to scale Everest.

Leonardo Di Caprio and Kate Winslett were in *Titanic* (captained in real life by Hanley-born Edward Smith). *LA Confidential* was one of the best films of the year. And Steve Coogan introduced us to the hilarious Alan Partridge.

Stoke on Trent was granted unitary authority status, enabling our council to control more local functions. And Stoke Rep Theatre opened its new site in Leek Road.

1998/99 Season: Division 2

"this is Staffordshire" website launched

We tend to remember things that are different; things that attract our attention. Have a boring month at work, where each day slowly grinds into the next, and the only thing you're likely to remember was you constantly checking whether your watch had stopped.

But if something different happened you could – depending on how different it was – remember it forever. Well, this season was like watching the decorators come in on the first week of the month and paint your office. That's a bit different and about as exciting as work sometimes gets. Then you spent the rest of the month watching the paint dry.

I know we went through all the same match day rituals as we were (still are) season ticket holders and went to every game.

We would've bought the latest *Oatcake* on the way to the ground. We would've still been getting used to the cold plastic seats in the less than half-full, or more than half-empty (you choose) new-ish stadium. We would've seen the chewing-gum and fag ends clogging up the troughs in the gents. We would've clapped the lads onto the pitch, cheered every goal, moaned at every decision that went against us and groaned when we conceded. We would've practised ignoring the away fans when their team scored or when we lost.

Yep; we must've done all these things, but I'm jiggered if I can remember much about this season as its over-riding characteristic was blandness.

Most of the opposing teams looked like the same uninspired outfit to me. For all I know, it could've been the same set of players in different strips each time.

Brian Little

Brian Little became the fifth man to call himself the Stoke City manager in the last 16 months.

He came with a good pedigree. He was a former England international who had starred in the top Division with Villa and, since hanging up his boots, had had some success as a manager.

Little brought in Short and Small as wing-backs and *(bad joke alert)* Stoke fans waited eagerly for the signing of a 'keeper called Large, a winger called Quick and a striker called Hyma Scoringsensation. But they all turned us down.

But an Aussie named David Oldfield accepted our offer and was drafted into centre-midfield.

Brian was the latest of a line of high-profile managers given the task of achieving success for Stoke on the pitch. And this time it looked like it might well happen. We kicked off the season with six straight wins.

In fact, by the end of November '98 we'd won fourteen and drawn one of our first twenty games. We looked absolute certainties for the play-offs, if not automatic promotion.

But this is Stoke we're on about and our form then crashed like a hundred big greenhouses in an earthquake, before being hit by a train. And then another train.

And the fans gawped in disbelief as we went on to win only seven of our last 26 games.

We finished the season in 8th place, seven points short of the play-offs and 32 points behind Fulham who went up as champions.

As for the Cups, we went out of the League Cup in Round 1 and the FA Cup in Round 2. Enough said.

Then Brian Little left Stoke at the end of the season and we awaited our sixth manager in just over two years.

James O'Connor and Clive Clarke

The appearance of these two young Irish lads was the undoubted highlight of the season. James was a fiery little midfield dynamo and Clive showed some quality at left-back.

Both went on to serve the club well over several seasons.

"google it"

Bill Clinton and Monica Lewinsky were in the news. Google was founded in the US; an invention so good we now use the brand name as a verb.

The first episode of *Who Wants To Be A Millionaire* was aired on ITV and Sky Sports News was launched.

Tom Hanks demonstrated his versatility again in *Saving Private Ryan,* and Brad Pitt and Ed Norton were in *Fight Club*.

The career of Longton-born actor Freddie Jones featured in the Telegraph and the Sentinel's website was launched.

<u>1999/2000 Season: Division 2</u>

Regent Theatre in Hanley re-opened by the Queen

"Try as I might", said Boris Johnson, reflecting on his decision to leave his job as a management consultant after only one week, "I could not look at an overhead projection of a growth profit matrix and stay conscious".

But our new chairman Gunnar Gislarsson and his Icelandic chums seemed to have had no such problem.

They had pooled their money to buy a controlling interest in Stoke City because they were certain that by getting us promoted to the Premier League within five years the value of the club would rocket. And their "growth profit matrix" (whatever that is) would make happy reading for the men from the land of fire and ice.

But theirs wasn't the first brave move we'd seen at Stoke this season. John Rudge had severed his long-time connections with the Vale to become our Director of Football (whatever that is).

And Gary Megson had become our sixth manager in just over two years. Given the average length of time the incumbents spent in the job we hoped the novel he'd bought to read during his lunch breaks wasn't a long one.

And, true to recent form, Gary had only been in the job for four months, winning 8, drawing 5 and losing 4 of his 17 games in charge before he was ousted to make way for the Icelanders' own man.

Gary's final game as our manager was the 1-1 draw with Tony Pulis's Bristol City at the Britannia Stadium.

Gudjon Thordarson

Gudjon had made a name for himself during a three year spell as the Icelandic national team manager when his teams won ten and drew four of 24 games. It was clear the Icelanders involved in the takeover had great faith in his ability to be a success in English football.

Gudjon himself had reportedly been instrumental in negotiating the takeover, and he was subsequently appointed as manager after it had gone through.

So Gary Megson was paid off and Gudjon set about bringing in his own players.

Chris Iwellumo & Brynjar Gunnarsson

Very big striker Chris (possibly spotted by John Rudge) had joined pre-season and defender/midfielder Brynjar was the most expensive, and arguably the best, of the boat full of Scandinavian players Gudjon signed that constituted the new Viking invasion.

Besides Gunnarsson, there was Mikel Hansen, and Frode Kippe. Then in March 2000 Gudjon's son, winger Bjarni Gudjonsson also joined us, although star striker Stickeet Onmeheadsson wisely refused to come on the grounds that bad jokes were likely to be made with his name.

Gudjon got off to a good start winning 5 and drawing 2 of his first eight games. We then had a poor spell, losing four of the next six games, winning only one. But we were in good form in the run-in winning nine, drawing four and losing only once.

Peter Thorne had had an outstanding season, scoring 30 goals which included three hat-tricks. But we had to settle for the play-offs due to a 6th place finish, scoring 68 against 42.

Then we had to face the disappointment of losing to Gillingham in the play-offs, especially as some of the refereeing decisions that went against us were hard to stomach.

But we did have some consolation by winning a trophy this season.

"We won it two times..."

We maintained our 100% record at Wembley in the club's third appearance there by beating Bristol City 2-1, with goals by Thorney and Kav, in front of a crowd of over 75,000. Although we'd won the Autoglass Trophy for the second time, what the fans really wanted was to get out of this Division. But this season's average crowd of only 11,246 indicated that a lot of Stokies doubted the club was going the right way about it.

Sir Stan dies

On 23rd February 2000, Sir Stanley Matthews, one of Stoke's greatest sons and one of the world's greatest footballers, died. Tens of thousands lined the streets of the Potteries and thousands more were in the Britannia for the farewell drive-past of Sir Stan's cortege on 3rd March.

His service took place at St Peter's church in Stoke.

2000/01 Season: Division 2

Still 40,000 employed in the Pottery

and allied industries

Who hasn't thought of themselves as a Stoke player, or as the manager, or even as the owner of the club?

We wouldn't think we could do a better job than an electrician, or a surgeon, or a tailor, or an airline pilot, butcher, baker or candlestick maker, but one of the peculiarities of football (and politics) is we usually believe that, given the chance, we could.

The Icelanders had put their money where their mouths were to prove that they could do a better job of running a club. And this being their second season in charge, they probably expected promotion this time round as part of their five year plan.

But "thinking is easy", said the German writer Goethe, "acting is difficult, and to put one's thoughts into action is the most difficult thing in the world".

Wayne Thomas

Defender Wayne Thomas (probably another one spotted by John Rudge) joined from Torquay pre-season for £200K and looked a good prospect, able to play at either centre-back or full-back.

But the emphasis was still on Scandinavian players. So the likes of winger Stefan Thordarson, 'keeper Birkir Kristinsson and striker Rikki Dadasson, reportedly tracked by several top clubs, all followed as well. And Arnar Gunlargsson kept flitting on and off the radar as a loan player. We were one of the big spenders of this Division.

The League campaign

Like last season, we had an unusually good goal difference, scoring 74 against 49, Peter Thorne finishing as top scorer with 19. We had 4-goal wins over Oxford, Peterborough, Bristol Rovers and Swindon.

But again, like last season, our form wasn't consistent enough. It wasn't helped by the constant influx of new players who had to adapt to the pace and power of the English game. But the new faces stimulated interest and the average gates rose to 13,767, although, in contrast, less than 9,000 turned up at the Vale to see the derby end in a draw.

We finished fifth in the table, only one place better than last year; so we had to settle for the play-offs again, but we never looked like getting past Walsall.

We drew the first leg 1-1 at our place before collapsing 4-2 at theirs. This was a bad result for all of us and I'd imagine a big set-back for the Icelanders' five year plan, which was now probably running behind schedule.

Cup fiasco

One of the things you look forward to when you're in a lower Division is a home draw in the Cup to one of the big teams. They'll probably "rest" one or two of their stars rather than risk their limbs playing against what they'll see as a bunch of hoofers and cloggers in Nowheresville. And there's the prospect we could catch them on a day they don't fancy it while our lads are ready to be unleashed for the kill. And the television people start looking us up on Wiki so they know where to send the camera crew.

And so it was when we came out of the hat to play Liverpool at the Brit. The Icelanders would've been rubbing their hands at the sight of a full house. And when Thorney hit the inside of their post in the second minute the television and radio commentators (I'm guessing, because I wiped the tape without watching it when I got home) probably said something like "And now Liverpool really know they've got a game on their hands!".

And that might've been the last time we got in their half, for all I remember. There was some gallows humour ("we're gonna win 5-4") from the Boothen End when we were 4-0 down before half-time, but we'd all felt like the life had been drained out of us when it finished 8-0.

Then the Icelanders spent the money they'd made from the game on new striker Andy Cooke.

More jobs lost

Russell Crowe was *Gladiator*. *Shrek* was one of the best family films and Owen Wilson went *Behind Enemy Lines*.

The Office made its debut on TV and reflected the craziness of the workplace. *Blackadder Goes Forth* series was hilarious.

More than five million mobile phones were sold over the Christmas period, but 900 jobs were lost at the Michelin in another blow to our area.

2001/02 Season: Division 2

Census shows reduced Stoke on Trent population

Stoke were one of the big clubs in this Division and probably the biggest movers in the transfer market. But the irony was that no matter how many new players came in, the team's final position in the table barely changed in three seasons.

In Gudjon's first season in charge we finished 6th with a goal difference of plus 26. In his second season we finished 5th with a goal difference of plus 25. And this season we finished 5th again with a goal difference of plus 27.

Shtaniuk, Handyside and Hoekstra

Graham Kavanagh had joined Cardiff for £1M pre-season. And Peter Thorne followed him for £1.7M after only five games, in which he scored four goals.

These moves prompted some unrest amongst the fans, especially as Thorney and Kav were top players at this level, and they'd moved to a rival club.

But Gudjon pulled a rabbit out of the hat by bringing in classy and teak-tough Belarusian centre-back Sergei Shtaniuk and footballing centre-back Peter Handyside to partner him and captain the team.

And former Ajax winger Peter Hoekstra was another cracking signing for this level. Tall, gangly, with a great touch and almost unplayable on his day, Hooky became a crowd favourite.

Also coming out of the minibus into the New Arrivals lounge at the Brit were goalkeeper Neil Cutler, Belgian midfielder Jurgen Van Deurzen and Petur Marteinsson, an Icelandic defender who had the misfortune to break his ankle before he'd even arrived in Stoke. A goalkeeper called Jani Viander signed for a big fee but I can't remember ever seeing him between the sticks, while African striker Souleymane Oulare (Gudjon's "Jimmy Ffloyd Hasselbank") didn't feature much more due to an illness after he'd signed.

Then just when we thought the minibus had emptied, 'keeper Gavin Ward, striker Deon Dublin and midfielders Tony Dinning and Ian Brightwell got out as well.

Bearing in mind this "Second Division" we were playing in at the time was actually the third tier of English football, the Board would've expected to see their investment reflected in results. And there were a couple of 5-goal wins over Wycombe and Cambridge and a 4 goal win over Bury, all at the Brit.

But they would've also been disappointed at our failure to clinch automatic promotion; we had to settle for the play-offs – again. So we all stocked up on toilet rolls before we had to face Cardiff over two legs of the semi-finals. And when they won the first leg 2-1 at Stoke the advantage was with the Bluebirds. Then something amazing happened.

"What does 'fortuitous' mean, dad?"

In the 93rd minute of the second leg, with the score at 0-0, meaning Cardiff were leading on aggregate, James O'connor scored what was probably the most important goal of his Stoke career. Then the ref blew his whistle for 30 minutes of extra time. We weren't at the match; we were huddled round the radio in our living room, but we could read in Nigel's commentary that Stoke believed they could win.

Fortune supposedly favours the brave, so what happened next must've left the Stoke players feeling like the bravest dudes on the planet. Thrown on as a late substitute by Gudjon, the rarely-seen Souleymane Oulare deflected a James O'Connor free kick and the ball flew into the Cardiff net past their wrong-footed 'keeper.

The wild celebrations among the 600 Stokies in the stadium were echoed by tens of thousands more in living rooms in North Staffordshire and beyond. After that, the final against Brentford seemed a breeze and Gudjon had finally won promotion at the third attempt.

Then something else amazing happened. Within hours of clinching promotion, Gudjon was sacked by the Icelandic owners.

It was a brave move, but it soured the atmosphere and split the fans — one group going as far as lobbying for Gudjon's reinstatement. But the decision had been made; there was no going back and the club was looking for yet another new manager.

9/11

The horrific attacks occurred on New York's Twin Towers. *Spiderman* was in the film charts and Britney in the music charts.

The average cost of a terraced house in Stoke on Trent was just over £30K.

2002/03 Season: Division 1

Stoke on Trent has its first elected Mayor

The Icelandic owners must've felt like they'd trodden on every crack in the pavements, broken a few mirrors and had their paths crossed by an extended family of black cats.

After sacking Gudjon they had appointed Steve Cotterill, only for him to leave us after 13 games in charge to become Sunderland's assistant manager.

So Gunnar asked former Stoke midfielder Dave Kevan to hold the reins temporarily as our caretaker manager.

Dave was in charge for four games, losing all of them, before we saw yet another new manager drafted in.

Tony Pulis

It looked for a while like George Burley might become our next manager but, for whatever reason, he didn't.

But Tony Pulis did. And none of us were aware at the time how important Tony was going to become for the future of our club.

In fact he got off to a dismal start losing his first four games (so the team had lost eight in a row). And it was his tenth game in charge before we recorded a win.

We actually dropped into the relegation zone at one point after a 6-0 defeat at Forrest, and that was the catalyst for Tony to take radical steps to change things around.

Mark Crossley and Ade Akinbiyi

Mark was a terrific new signing, a sound 'keeper and an inspirational character who got his team-mates to bond as a unit on the pitch.

Ade also joined and was a goalscoring muscle-bound power-house who troubled defenders by his pace and eagerness to dominate that dangerous channel between the centre circle and the opposition's goal.

Ade effectively replaced Chris Greenacre, who had been signed by Cotterill for a big fee.

And winger Kris Commons was developing into a good player on the left flank and featured increasingly in the first team.

We eventually saw the improvement in form we needed to claw ourselves away from the relegation zone. We lost only twice in the next dozen games and went into our final game, at home to Reading, needing a win to ensure we stayed up.

It had taken four years to get out of the Division below us and we were desperate not to return there. So there was a huge sense of relief when an Ade Akinbiyi goal was enough to beat Reading at the Brit.

We finished 21st in the table, avoiding relegation by one place.

This Division had proved a lot harder than the one we'd struggled to get out of, but we were now guaranteed at least another year at this level and it looked like the managerial position had been sorted, at least for now.

Five year plans

In the days of Stalin's USSR officials were shot if they failed to achieve their five year plan. But our workplace, with all its H&S malarkey nowadays, is a much safer place. All over Britain there were businesses and organisations - our club being one of them - setting themselves demanding schedules, but nobody was expected to get shot if these weren't met.

But that didn't mean Tony Pulis was getting an easy ride as manager of our club. For a start, Stoke didn't look (to me anyway) like a club heading for promotion to the Premier League. And that was supposedly a key component of the plan.

And some fans were vociferously critical of the style of play.

We'd all hoped that the Icelanders' five year plan would succeed. They had seemingly put a lot of their own money into the club and it would've been win-win all round if they pulled it off. But after most of four seasons in charge, it now looked unlikely.

Ceramica

The allies invaded Iraq.

The first of the Bourne trilogy, *The Bourne Identity*, was released. Tom Cruise was *The Last Samurai* and Russell Crowe was *Master and Commander*.

Angus Deayton made the news. *Foyle's War* started on TV.

And Ceramica opened in Burslem.

2003/04 Season: Division 1

Trentham Gardens re-opens to the public

Our six seasons at the Britannia Stadium so far had been a rollercoaster ride. A total of nine managers had overseen relegation in our first season, a disastrous implosion of form in the second, gut-wrenching play-off defeats in the third and fourth, an improbable promotion in the fifth and us narrowly avoiding relegation in the sixth.

That's fine for the adrenalin-junkies, but these experiences had understandably taken their toll on the rest of us.

People were ageing beyond their years. Some teenaged lads in the Boothen End had taken to wearing cloth caps, tweed jackets and smoking pipes. Should nerve-tonics, old shag and hair dye now be on offer along with beer, burgers and chips at the food outlets? Nah; probably not.

So this season we needed a period of calm; to be lulled into a sense of security with a comfortable mid-table finish. And that's what we got.

GNW, Daryl Russell & Ed de Goey

Sergei Shtaniuk returned to Russia, Peter Handyside retired from professional football, and James O'Connor, Chris Iwellumo, Brynjar Gunnarsson, Petur Marteinsson and Neal Cutler all left the club.

So Tony started to bring in players he thought could help us consolidate at this level after last year's flirtation with relegation.

Ade Akinbyi returned on a permanent basis and was joined by his former Gillingham team-mate Carl Asaba. Combative central-midfielder John Eustace and right-midfielder Daryl Russell gave us bite and creativity in the middle of the park.

And two giants, six-foot seven-inch 'keeper Ed de Goey and forward Gifton Noel-Williams, were quintessentially Tony Pulis signings.

The team ethos looked like it was going to be one based on the size, power and determination of players who were also capable of decent football. And this was typically illustrated by the signing of centre-back Gerry Taggart who came, initially on loan, later in the season. Although Tony bucked the trend slightly when he brought in John Halls, a slim over-lapping full-back who looked to have bags of quality and potential.

The League campaign

After getting off to a good start with two wins (including an opening-day 3-0 victory at Derby) and two draws, our early season form went downhill and we were averaging exactly a point per game after twenty games.

But our form improved as a new team style emerged with the more games they played together. And the last 26 games averaged almost 2 points per game to ensure a final 11th place finish.

We had scored 58 against 55; Ade and GNW were joint top scorers with ten goals each. The average gate was up to 14,424. And for the first time in years we were content to sit back and let others sweat over the crucial final day placings for promotion and relegation.

But our Cup form was abysmal. We went straight out of both competitions to Wimbledon and Gillingham.

Goal of the Season

It was the first season that Stoke had held this competition and it was won by a thunderous Peter Hoekstra left-foot strike that arrowed into the top corner. It was his second goal in a hat-trick against Reading at the Brit. Peter had rounded their 'keeper for his first and chipped the ball into the middle of the goal after their 'keeper had guessed wrongly when he scored his third with a penalty.

Hooky was in fantastic form for this game and had we heard news of the Reading defenders being treated for feelings of confusion, disorientation and dizzy spells afterwards it would've come as no surprise.

Stoke Marathon at Trentham Gardens

Facebook was launched.

Arnold Schwarenegger was sworn in as Governor of California. Tom Cruise starred in *Collateral,* but *The Lord of the Rings – The Return of the King* and *Shrek 2* topped the film charts.

Black Eyed Peas, Peter Andre and Britney topped the singles charts. Derren Brown played Russian roulette. *Little Britain* and *Strictly Come Dancing* were new to television.

Actor and singer Adam Faith died in a hotel while visiting Stoke. And long traffic delays resulted from the updating of the A500 road works.

2004/05 Season: The Championship

The Italian Gardens at Trentham

opened by the Duke of York

The relative peace and stability that came with last season's mid-table finish was just an interlude, a breather; the calm before the storm.

"A wise man in times of peace prepares for war", said the Roman poet Horace.

And that's as true for each of us when preparing for the challenges, skirmishes and battles we will inevitably face in our daily lives as it is for governments planning for the longer term.

Fate is a pit-bull that likes to bite you in the arse just when you've settled into the hammock of contentment and all seems well with the world.

And it's particularly true for the inhabitants of the volatile and unpredictable realm of football management.

The original five year plan for promotion to the Premier League had had to be revised again as Stoke ended this season with a mid-table finish in the Championship. But at least some of the absent Stoke fans were returning as our average gate had risen to 16,456 (over 5,000 more than Gudjon's first season).

So it didn't come as a huge surprise when the Board gave Tony a new one-year contract.

But it *did* come as a huge surprise (although Horace might've seen this coming) when, only four weeks later, events took a weird twist and the Board sensationally sacked Tony at the end of this season.

Simonson, Duberry and Brammer

Steady-Eddie 'keeper Steve Simonson had come in from Everton and became our regular between the sticks. Michael Duberry was drafted in to become the centre-back partner for Gerry Taggart, who returned on a permanent basis.

And Dave Brammer joined as a centre-midfield play-maker.

The League: "What does 'binary' mean, dad?"

Of seventeen consecutive games between October 2004 and February 2005 fifteen had a scoreline of 1-0 and two finished 0-0. In fact the only significant spike in the graph of this season's scores was when we got hammered 6-3 at Crystal Palace, a game in which we conceded almost a sixth of the 38 goals we let in all year.

Only promoted Wigan conceded fewer goals. And only relegated Rotherham scored fewer than our measly tally of 36. It was that kind of season.

We had actually got off to a good start and were sitting top of the table after eight games.

But teams with the goals for / against ratio we had this season are destined to exist in that mid table wilderness where tumbleweed replaces the drama of a promotion campaign or relegation battle.

Our constant struggle to score meant opposition teams could come to the Brit with some confidence and attack us. And they did; we lost ten home games, one less than we lost on our travels.

We had good wins over Derby, Sunderland and West Brom. Gifton finished as top scorer with 13 (more than a third of our total) and Dave Brammer's screamer against Leicester won the Goal of the Season award.

The Cups

It looked like the possibility of an upset in the 3rd Round of the FA Cup which, unusually, saw us doing the upsetting this time by going ahead with a Wayne Thomas goal at Arsenal.

But the Gunners came back to win 2-1, which happened to be the same score we lost to Oldham at their place in the League Cup.

The Man in Black

youtube is launched. And the horrific Hurricane Katrina devastated New Orleans.

Joaquin Phoenix was brilliant as Johnny Cash in *Walk The Line*. *The X Factor* and *Mock The Week* made their television debuts.

Ken Dodd was on at the Regent Theatre and we all had to extend our car parking tickets or delay our taxis - as usual.

Tunstall Park held a carnival and a Visitor Survey showed that people felt welcome when visiting the Potteries.

2005/06 Season: The Championship

Monkey Forrest opened and

A500 'D Road' updates completed

Although we didn't know it at the start, this was the last season for which the Icelandic owners would be in charge.

They once again turned to someone with no previous experience in English football and brought in Dutchman Johann Boskamp to manage the club following the sacking of previous incumbent Tony Pulis.

Johann certainly had a different style to Tony.

And I don't mean that one wore what looked like a big chunky cardigan while the other wore a track-suit and baseball cap. No; it went beyond that superficial level.

Different management styles are one of the things that make football the fascinating spectacle it is, and Johann's was probably as different to Tony's as you could get.

And so we all climbed aboard again for the next leg of the magical mystery tour.

Mama Sidibie

Tony's last act before getting the sack was to sign 'Big Mama', a striker he'd had in the side at his former club Gillingham.

And Johann played Mama 42 times this season.

Carl Hoefkens and Sammy Bangoura

A Belgian international, Carl was quick and versatile, able to play at centre-back or full back. With his instinct to drive forward when in possession he had the look of an old fashioned inside forward who'd been converted to play as a defender.

Sammy, on the other hand, was unmistakably an out-and-out striker. He'd cost the club a record fee of, depending on which report you read, either £1M or a million Euros. Fortunately for Stoke and their owners at the time, that matched the fee we received for the transfer of reserve 'keeper Ben Foster to Manchester United.

And when he started rattling in the goals, Sammy looked a bargain. But when he failed to return to Stoke on schedule after international duty and a pre-season break, we all wondered what was going on.

The League campaign

We drew our opening game, and that was the *only* draw in our first 27 games, with us winning twelve and losing fourteen of the remainder. And that wasn't the only strange thing about our form. By the end of the season we'd won only seven games at home, losing eleven. But we'd won ten away from home, also losing eleven.

Which is why some subscribe to the theory that the fans who followed Stoke home and away have rosier memories of this season than the majority who only attended home games.

We had been up to 5th in the table just before Christmas, but things then fell away badly and we won only five of our final

22 games. Loan striker Paul Gallagher had finished as top scorer with 12, and Dave Brammer again won the Goal of the Season award, this time with a cracker against Luton.

By the end of the season a combination of factors must've persuaded the Icelanders to call it a day. The team had finished 13th, one place lower than last season, and average crowds had fallen to 14,738. They had put a lot of money into Stoke in recent years and now their hopes of making money out of the club's progress must've more or less evaporated.

And there had been what looked like an almighty bust-up involving Boskamp, his assistant Jan de Koning and John Rudge over some incident or other.

Coates and Pulis return

The Icelanders then re-sold their shares back to Peter Coates, now seemingly a much richer man. Peter brought Tony Pulis back as manager, and we all argued about what it meant for the future of our club.

Unity House

Twitter is launched. Will it be yet another innovation where the unexpected consequences of its use will exceed the expected?

Di Caprio and Nicholson were brilliant in *The Departed*. And *Borat* was another highly original Sacha Baron Cohen character who made us cringe and laugh.

And only thirty-odd years after it was opened, the city's tallest building, Unity House, was demolished.

2006/07 Season: The Championship

Smoking banned in public places

When the salesman responded to the customer's question "would you buy one of these yourself?" with the answer "I'd sell one to my own grandmother", it was a reminder of how we each see things from our unique perspective.

And it's from this that our opinions are formed; you'll never find two people on the planet who have identical views on *everything*. But there will be plenty who share the same opinion on something.

And so it was when opinions were divided on the return of Peter Coates as chairman and Tony Pulis as manager.

There was quite a debate amongst the fans about whether the return of the two men was the best thing for our club, although there was a recognition that both had shown guts and a willingness to make a personal sacrifice to return to their former roles. Strong views were voiced either side with others sitting somewhere between. Time would tell.

Danny Higginbotham and Lee Hendrie

Former England international Lee was a creative midfielder whose unmistakable class made an immediate impact when he came on loan a couple of months into the season, making his debut in the memorable 4-0 win at Leeds.

Danny had come in pre-season for a bargain fee of £225K. And it was no surprise when he was made team captain as his leadership qualities were evident from the off.

Ric

I'm guessing that I wasn't the only one who'd never heard of Ricardo Fuller before he signed for us. He'd apparently done the rounds at Crystal Palace, Hearts, Preston, Portsmouth, Ipswich and Southampton.

So it was all the more surprising when this relatively unknown player turned out to be, on his day, one of the most exciting strikers to have pulled a Stoke shirt over his head.

Ric comes second only to the great Sir Stan on my list for the "Making Something Out Of Nothing" Award. And that's an astonishing achievement for a bloke who probably could have walked past me unrecognised in the Potteries Shopping Centre the week before he signed for us.

The League campaign

After an indifferent start with only one win in our first ten games our form picked up dramatically with nine wins in the next twelve games. But it was our poor start and some later inconsistency that ultimately cost us at least a shot at promotion through the play-offs. We finished in eighth place.

The same team that could win 4-0 at Leeds, beat Norwich 5-0 and Cardiff 3-0 also managed to lose heavily at Colchester and throw away a 2-0 lead to lose at Preston. But that's football, and this is Stoke we're on about.

But overall, the omens were encouraging. We were looking good at both ends of the pitch, scoring 62 goals and conceding only 41. And average attendances had risen to nearly 16,000.

Andy Griffin was back again and scored the Goal of the Season with a tremendous right-foot strike at the Boothen End in a cold, misty evening game against Coventry which was shown live on television.

Progress Report

Although we hadn't wasted much time in getting knocked out of the domestic Cup competitions, the League campaign had been promising and there were signs of a decent squad coming together.

We'd lost only three home games all season, compared to 11 last season and 10 the year before that.

The quality of the football had been more entertaining and, with some targeted investment, there were grounds for optimism.

"Heads go up..."

Gordon Brown became Prime Minister. World renowned footballer Ferenc Puskas died.

The final *Harry Potter* book was published and became the fastest selling book in history.

Local man John Caudwell sold his mobile phone business for a huge £1.5 billion.

The government enacted a law banning smoking in public places.

And Radio Stoke's Nigel Johnson commentated on his fifteen-hundredth game in March 2007.

2007/08 Season: The Championship

Britannia Stadium bought by the club

When a club has been out of top flight football for as long as Stoke had you kind of get used to it. But you never fully get used to it.

For the older fans who saw the great teams of the sixties and seventies slugging it out toe-to-toe with the top clubs the Championship could be a fairly uninspiring Second Division.

And for the younger fans the reminiscences of the older fans are about as relevant as granny going on about being rationed to one egg a week during the war.

But the excitement of this season's promotion campaign, the prospect of Premier League football next year and the emergence of the inspirational Pottermouth, brought everybody together. The atmosphere was now as good as it had been for a quarter of a century.

Liam Lawrence and Rory Delap

Although both had joined last season it was this time round they made their impact. Liam was a creative wide player rather than a traditional winger, and his 15 goals saw him finish with Ric as joint top scorer this season.

Rory was a solid holding central-midfielder who had the misfortune to break his leg on his home debut. But he made a full recovery and through what would become a nationally renowned exocet missile of a throw-in, Rory probably put more dangerous centres into the box than most wingers.

Leon Cort became the club's record signing and, as well as being a decent centre-back, scored eight valuable goals. Danny Pugh was Mr Dependability; he always seemed to perform to the same good standard whenever drafted in regardless of the length of time he'd been out of the team. Richard Cresswell was an ever-present who played most of the season in an unfamiliar wing role, but still scored a crucial dozen goals. And Glenn Whelan came in for the second half of the season and added to the passing and shooting range from midfield.

Ryan

Rarely does a young player come in to a side and make a consistently exceptional impact throughout his first season, but Ryan Shawcross did. A traditional centre-back; tall, and still growing, he arrived initially on loan and you'd be hard pressed to find a Stoke supporter who didn't think Tony Pulis had pulled off a masterstroke when Ryan eventually signed permanently from Manchester United for a give-away £2M. This classy defender became a mainstay of our back-four, scored vital goals and looked easily capable of stepping up to the Premier League.

The League campaign

With only six wins in our first seventeen games the odds on Stoke gaining automatic promotion after our 0-0 draw at Burnley at the end of November '07 must've been long.

Then our form changed and things looked up like a man standing near the Eiffel Tower as we won fifteen and drew ten of our last 29 games.

There were the inevitable incontinence-inducing moments during the run-in, like when we unexpectedly lost at home to Crystal Palace. But we were back on track a week later when we came from behind to win 2-1 at Coventry with goals from Ric and Liam. Then Mama's two goals (the second one resembling a Ric solo effort) not only won us the game against Bristol City at the Brit, but also effectively put one of our rivals out of the race. And Cresser's winner a week later at Colchester meant we needed only a point from our final game.

"Do eet Pulis, please do eet"

Is it true that the Stoke players plastered their faces with red war paint, wrestled with wild boars and ate a diet of raw meat after listening to Pottermouth's inspirational battle-cry before our final game against Leicester? I don't know, but I guess it must be.

In the event we got a nervy goal-less draw, but it was enough. So after 23 years outside the top flight, with a similar number of managerial changes during that time, Pulis and the lads did eet. We were finally returning to play the overpaid prima donnas in front of full houses.

Banks in trouble

The Northern Rock Bank had to be nationalised.

Leo Di Caprio and Russell Crowe were excellent in *Body of Lies*, *The Simpsons Movie* hit the big screen and Stephen Fry toured America in a London taxi. Duffy topped the singles charts for five weeks with *Mercy* and there was an All-nighter of Soul music at the Kings Hall in Stoke.

2008/09 Season: The Premier League

Woolworths shops closed around Potteries

Most football pundits seemed to think that Stoke's chances of surviving more than one season in the Premier League were slightly less than Britain's creditors saying we didn't need to repay our national debt.

Hell, there was even a joke going round among Stoke fans about Tony being confident of keeping us up for three seasons – autumn, winter and spring.

But like the bookie who'd paid out after only one game to those punters who'd bet we'd get relegated, they had overlooked something important. Stoke were no longer the soft touch that many thought us to be.

We had a manager with determination, drive and a passionate single-mindedness to succeed.

We had a group of players with more talent than they'd been given credit for, and a point to prove.

And we had supporters who generated a noise and a passion that turned a bog standard stadium into a gladiatorial arena that cowered many opponents.

Now we'd got here we were going to stay for a while, like it or not.

Sorensen, Faye, Etherington and Wilkinson

Tommy was a free agent after being released by Villa. He signed for us after a pre-season trial and went on to become our regular 'keeper, and showed Villa that they'd made a big mistake.

Cashing in on others' mistakes is part of the game and we did it again when we snapped up Abdy Faye from Newcastle and Sunderland allowed Danny Higginbotham to return to Stoke.

Dave Kitson and Seyi Olofinjana were the big-money signings. And local lad Andy Wilkinson became a crowd favourite with his whole-hearted, gritty and determined style.

And the quality of the squad was further enhanced when striker James Beattie and terrific winger Matthew Etherington joined us in the January transfer window.

The League campaign

It wasn't Liam's penalty, our first Premier League goal at the Brit that triggered it. Nor was it Ric's fantastic solo effort which put us 2-1 up. It was our 94th minute winner that did it, with the scores standing at 2-2 and Villa having levelled twice.

The place erupted. The noise couldn't have been more deafening and the celebrations more manic among the 25,000 Stoke fans in the stadium had they been given an extra month's paid holiday with a supermodel of their choice.

And that, according to some experts, was more likely to happen than Mama knocking in the winner with his right ear off a Rory Delap long throw.

We had to wait two months for our next win, but then we collected the scalps of Spurs, Sunderland, Arsenal and West Brom within the space of five weeks.

143

Then, incredibly, we went another two months without a win and those who had written us off found their voices again, but they still hadn't learned much. Our seven wins and three draws in our final fifteen games saw us finish in a comfortable mid-table position and the tone of many of the commentators changed to one of genuine respect for what Stoke had achieved.

Ric, looking a class act at this level, finished as top scorer with eleven goals, including the Goal of the Season Award for his stunner against Villa in our first game at the Brit.

And the average gate of 26,954 was our highest since the 1974/75 season and bettered only seven times in the club's history.

The Cups

Although we made it to the Quarter Finals of the Carling Cup we shot ourselves in the foot and lost the home tie to Derby. And a second string side lost 2-0 at Hartlepool in R3 of the FA Cup. Enough said.

Giant Observation Wheel opened at Trentham

The bankruptcy of Lehman Brothers Bank was the biggest in US history and had knock-on effects around the world. Daniel Craig put in a good performance in *Defiance*, as did Liam Neeson in *Taken*, and Heath Ledger won a posthumous Oscar for *Dark Night*.

The Christmas day *Wallace and Gromit* and *The X Factor Results* were the most watched TV shows in Britain.

And our own version of the London Eye opened at Trentham.

144

2009/10 Season: The Premier League

Stoke on Trent Centenary 31st March 1910 – 2010

The pressure was on: lots of clubs had shown that it was easier reaching the Premier League than staying there.

So this is the time when a manager has to use every scrap of his initiative and imagination to overcome the legendary pitfalls of "the second season syndrome".

Tony Pulis had already brought in Gerry "the mullet" Francis to help out with the training and shortened the pitch to the minimum permitted size. Would he now get the hippo to wind up the opposition by doing keepy-uppy with a beach ball in front of their dugout? Nah; probably not.

But we were no longer the shock troops of the Premier League. And the physical power of our play and the use of Rory's Rocket would catch fewer teams out this time round.

And the fans that went home knackered after every home game last season were unlikely to recreate the same levels of raucous passion that previously cowed so many of the opposition.

So Tony knew that he had to continue to bring in good quality players who could compete at this level. And one of the best measures of progress is the strength of the line-up we now had on the bench which, with seven substitutes and an assortment of coaches, trainers and the Chief Assistant to the Assistant Chief Trainer, looked like it'd been lifted from Hanley Bus Station.

Huth, Tuncay and Begovic

Seyi Olifinjana left pre-season, and Richard Cresswell and Leon Cort followed him out of the club in January. But Rock-solid German international defender Robert Huth and Turkish international striker Tuncay, a player with some flair, both came in from Middlesborough.

Defender Danny Collins and midfield dynamo Dean Whitehead arrived from Sunderland, and highly-rated Bosnian 'keeper Asmir Begovic joined from Pompey.

The League campaign

Looking back over some previous seasons it's noticeable how we often follow a pattern of winning a good proportion of our points over a number of consecutive games, or we go through a stretch from which we get very little.

This was one of those seasons. We were out of the starting blocks well with four wins and four draws from our first eleven games, losing only to Chelsea (after we'd taken the lead), Man United and Liverpool.

Then we went through a spell during November and December where our sole win in eight games was a narrow 1-0 over Pompey at the Brit.

By the end of December we were at the mid-point of the season with only five wins under our belts. And one of those had been an against-all-odds affair when a great run by Ric and fine finish by Glenn Whelan saw us chalk up an improbable 1-0 win at the club named after local knight Harry Hotspur.

Then we hit a good spell of form in the second half of the season winning six and drawing eight of our last nineteen games. We had good away wins at Pompey, Fulham and West Ham, and creditable draws against the likes of Liverpool, Villa, Everton and Man City.

And we were only denied 3 points against Mancini's men after the Ref later admitted he'd wrongly ruled out what would've been our injury time winner. Five of the six games we lost were against the top clubs.

So we defied the odds again by finishing with 47 points, putting us in 11th place - one better than last season.

And our goal difference of minus 14 tells a different story when you look behind the statistic. Eleven of these goals were actually conceded in our last two away games at Chelsea and Man United.

The Cups

After a great come-back to beat Blackpool 4-3 we went out of the League Cup following a 4-0 implosion at Portsmouth. But we reached the Quarter Finals of the FA Cup for the first time since 1972, collecting the scalps of Arsenal and Man City along the way. But we missed good chances at Chelsea and bowed out at 2-0.

"Staffordshire Hoard"

More than 53,000 people visited the Potteries Museum in 23 days to see the Anglo-Saxon gold treasure discovered in a Staffordshire farmer's field.

And Charles and Camilla came to celebrate our Centenary.

2010/11 Season: The Premier League

FA Cup History

If we had to field a second-string side against Barcelona at the Nou Camp I'd still expect us to scrape a narrow win. It's because, like the man who wrote to the MOD claiming that he must've been abducted by aliens as he'd lost an hour of his life the previous week, we can all be guilty of misjudgements on occasion. Then, after the match, I'd probably feel like he did when the MOD's response reminded him that that's when the clocks had gone forward.

It must've been the same for our critics (again) this season when they'd hoped their predictions of doom would be proved right. But Stoke comfortably retained their premiership status and made two historic visits to Wembley.

Jones, Pennant, Wilson & Walters

At £8M from Sunderland Kenwyne was our record signing. And to put that into perspective, £8M might well have exceeded the total amount Stoke had spent on players between 1863, when the club was formed, and the year 2000. But he still seemed good value for money at today's crazily inflated prices, finishing the season as joint top scorer with 12 goals and looking like a man with plenty of potential still to be realised.

Jermaine was one of those players who seemed to find his footballing "home" at Stoke after he'd spent time at Arsenal, Liverpool, Birmingham, in Spain and several other places on loan. We didn't have to wait long to see whether Tony could harness his talents: JP had a great season and Tony looked to have secured another quality signing.

With Dave Kitson and Liam Lawrence (plus cash) going the other way, Mark Wilson came in from Portsmouth to mixed expectations from Stoke fans unsure of his best position. But as the season unfolded it became increasingly clear that he was good on the ball with both feet and looked comfortable at full-back on either flank.

And while some Premier League managers were shelling out millions on strikers who looked like they couldn't hit a barn door from a yard out with a beach ball, Tony again demonstrated his ability to find quality in the bargain basement. Jon Walters came in from Championship Ipswich for a modest fee and we waited to see if he could take the step up. But by the end of the season "Super Jon" was not only a crowd favourite and joint top scorer with Kenwyne, he'd also scored a couple of goals that will live long in our collective memory.

The Cup Campaigns: history in the making

We beat Shrewsbury and Fulham in the early Rounds of the League Cup before going out to West Ham after extra time at their place.

But the FA Cup was a different story.

We started with a home tie against Cardiff; the kind of game pundits like to call "a potential banana skin". And after an uninspiring 1-1 draw most Stokies probably watched the televised replay through fingers and with the traditional pained expression.

Had we gone out of the Cup that night the Surprise-o-Meter would've twitched less than a few Premier League managers at the thought of signing our centre-backs. But we unexpectedly breezed through with a brace from Jon Walters before facing Wolves away in R4 where we won again, thanks to a header from Huthy and a penalty save from Tommy.

Then we hosted First Division table-toppers Brighton in R5. We were leading 3-0 by half-time and it stayed that way until the end with the Seagulls' fans amusing themselves with chants of "What's it like to see a pass?" Did they have a point? Should we, like some do, continually pass it sideways and backwards to increase our possession percentage? Nah.

We were in the Quarter Finals for the second year in succession and a home draw against West Ham gave us a real chance of making the semis for the first time since 1972, even though they'd just beaten us convincingly in the league at their place.

And despite a blatant handball before their goal we scraped through 2-1 in a cracking game. Then the celebrations continued as the word swept round the fans leaving the stadium that we'd avoided the Manchester clubs and drawn Bolton in the semi-final.

And a few weeks later, as Pete, Steve, Jen and I soaked up the atmosphere with 35,000 other Stokies outside the new Wembley stadium we were all in agreement that the semi was going to be a tight game, with probably the odd goal deciding it.

We had no idea — couldn't have had — that we were experiencing one of the best days of our lives as Stoke fans.

Well, as the American preacher who forecast the end of the world on 21st May could tell you, it's always possible that our predictions can be out a tad. The odd goal didn't settle it.

In the most one-sided FA Cup Semi Final since before the Second World War, shots from outside the box by Matt and Huthy, along with a great run by JP and finish by Kenwyne, had put us 3-0 up by half-time. And the TV bookmaker was offering 16/1 at the break for a 5-0 Stoke win.

Then Jon, with what was voted goal-of-the-season, halfway through the second half put us in an unassailable position. And some lucky punters must've been counting their winnings when he added another to seal an historic 5-0 victory.

I'm guessing that the pre-match odds of Stoke winning an FA Cup semi-final in such dramatic style would had been a bit less than those on us being first on Match of the Day every week from now on.

Historic first ever appearance in an FA Cup Final

Both Ric and Danny Higginbotham were now missing through long-term injury and our thin squad looked tired.

It seemed to me that too many of our lads were either carrying injuries or just didn't have enough left in the tank against a top squad assembled at a cost of hundreds of millions.

But there were no complaints from us as Man City ran out as worthy winners at 1-0; just pride in what had been achieved by Stoke in an historic FA Cup campaign.

The League Campaign

It was that kind of season: for a while it seemed like almost anyone outside the top six could go down, although we never looked in serious danger at any point. A slow start to the campaign saw us lose 2-1 at Wolves, where Kenwyne was carried off only minutes into his debut. Then Spurs took all three points at the Brit despite the MOTD cameras confirming we'd been denied a valid equaliser. And after we followed this up with a 2-0 defeat at Chelsea Big Al pointed out, with typical gallows humour, that this was a five goal improvement on last season's fixture. Three games and no points

But we all knew by now where our points were going to come from. Despite some notable exceptions – wins against Liverpool and Arsenal, along with home defeats to Blackpool and Wigan – the trend was otherwise predictable. Most of our points came from home games and against clubs outside the top six. And so it was no surprise when we chalked up ten on the board in our next four games against Villa (following Tony's courageous appearance on the day of his mother's death) West Ham, Newcastle and Blackburn, before going on to lose three on the road and then again at home to Manchester United.

And so it went on, with that trend being by no means exclusive to Stoke - which probably explains why the table was so tight that our defeat to Wigan on the last day saw us drop from a potential 8th to a final place of 13th.

Not as good a finish as we'd hoped, but we had secured the third season of survival in the top flight that Tony had planned for and demanded.

The incremental improvement in our playing and coaching staff and, as a consequence, of our play, was evident in the unusually large number of candidates this time round for Goal of the Season. It's ironic that a team which relies heavily on set-pieces should have provided us with so many top quality goals. But of the half-dozen or so I can think of, it was Ric's special to put us 2-0 up against Birmingham at the Brit which shaded it for me.

Stoke fan Adrian Lewis wins World Darts Championship

A massive earthquake killed thousands, moved the entire Japanese mainland by 2.4 metres and shifted the earth 10cm on its axis.

But much better news had come from South America where thirty-three Chilean miners were rescued alive after being stranded underground for 69 days. Anti-government protests ("The Arab Spring") spread throughout the Middle East.

Britain had its first coalition government since the Second World War and a royal wedding but, more importantly, England won The Ashes in Australia. Researchers found that our children are more likely to own a mobile phone than a book. And 'The King's Speech' did well at the Oscars.

A new superstore opened in Hanley. Local journalist John Abberley and radio presenter Sam Plank died within three months of each other.

And two former Stoke legends were in the news: Jimmy McIlroy was awarded an MBE and Terry Conroy made a remarkable recovery from a life-threatening illness.

<u>And finally...</u>

"So very difficult a matter it is", said the Greek historian Plutarch, "to trace and find out the truth of anything by history". But nearly 2,500 years ago he didn't have access to the Internet and Wikipedia, of course; things which I found invaluable as memory aides.

And no doubt any Stoke fan who decides to review the next fifty seasons in the year 2061 will have access to some as-yet undreamt of and spectacular technologies. It could be that by then we will have the scientific ability to copy the memories, thoughts and experiences which are stored chemically and electronically in our brains. These would then be mass-produced in the form of a pill (or pie – nobody likes taking pills) which, once ingested, provides the recipient with an instant memory bank of a lifetime of supporting Stoke, even though they might never have been to a game.

Too far-fetched? Maybe; but even if it were to happen it still wouldn't resolve what I think Plutarch was getting at when he spoke about the "truth". For what we regard as being "true" regarding football (as with most things) will be determined by our individual perceptions.

And while many of our perceptions as Stoke fans will overlap, each will essentially be unique, which is why we all come away from the same game with different opinions about what we've seen. And the truth from my perspective is that I've seen some great players and managers over the years.

But this is Stoke we're on about, and so there have been plenty more who've fallen short, some well-short, of greatness.

But "to find fault is easy", said Plutarch, "to do better may be difficult". I agree; owners, managers and players are all targets at different times for criticism, but much of this is just fans letting off steam and people in the game know this.

Owners are rarely popular, but a club needs them. The mega rich aside, how many of us would risk putting serious amounts of our own money into a football club?

And the job of being a manager – having to deal with fan expectations, the Board, coaching staff, players and the business of creating a winning team – is probably a task beyond most of us. For me, the four who've stood out and excelled in this ultra-demanding role in the last fifty seasons are (in chronological order) the very different Tony Waddington, Alan Durban, Lou Macari and Tony Pulis. Each of them grabbed the club by the scruff of the neck and dragged it forward.

And not all players can be stars. So long as a player has given everything when he's pulled the shirt over his head, then that's all we can ask for and expect. Let's face it; if we could do better then we'd be wearing the shirt instead.

The Board, manager and players we've now got in place (2011), I'm happy to say, is probably as good a set up as we've had in the past fifty years.

Long-term survival in the top flight, hopefully with a Cup thrown in, is now a realistic goal. And it's not often we could have said that in our time of following Stoke.

Now is a good time to be a Stoke fan. May it long continue.

Printed in Great Britain
by Amazon.co.uk, Ltd.,
Marston Gate.